*REMINISCENCES OF THE CRIMEAN CAMPAIGN.*

*Maull & Fox, 187a, Piccadilly.*]

MAJOR-GENERAL JOHN R. HUME.
*Commanded 55th Regiment from 1874 to 1879.*

# REMINISCENCES

OF THE

# CRIMEAN CAMPAIGN

*WITH THE 55th REGIMENT*

BY

JOHN R. HUME

*Major-General late 55th Regiment*

*Printed for the Author by*
UNWIN BROTHERS, 27, PILGRIM STREET
LUDGATE HILL, E.C.
1894

TO MY DEAR OLD FRIENDS AND COMRADES OF THE 55TH REGIMENT WHO SERVED IN THE CRIMEAN CAMPAIGN OF 1854 AND 1855, THESE REMINISCENCES, TAKEN FROM MY DIARY AND LETTERS, ARE INSCRIBED BY ONE WHO WAS PRESENT FROM THE COMMENCEMENT OF THE CAMPAIGN TO THE FALL OF SEBASTOPOL.

JOHN R. HUME,

*Major-General late* 55*th Regiment.*

# CONTENTS

## CHAPTER I.

55TH REGIMENT AT GIBRALTAR—WAR DECLARED—ORDERED TO THE EAST—PREPARATIONS—EMBARKATION—MALTA—DARDANELLES—CONSTANTINOPLE—SCUTARI—GOOD-BYE TO BROWN BESS—PARADES—REVIEWS—CRICKET . . . . 1

## CHAPTER II.

EMBARK FOR BULGARIA — VARNA—CARAGOULA—YURKSOKOVA — GAMES—CHOLERA — KOSLUDSHI—MARCH TO VARNA—EMBARK FOR CRIMEA ON BOARD THE "TIMANDRA"—GREAT FLOTILLA . 15

## CHAPTER III.

LANDING AT OLD FORT—FIRST NIGHT IN THE CRIMEA—MARCH TO THE BULGANAK—MARCH TO THE ALMA—BATTLE OF THE ALMA—AFTER THE BATTLE — CHOLERA — BIVOUAC AT THE KATCHA AND BELBEK—THE FAMOUS FLANK MARCH—BALACLAVA . . . . . 30

## CHAPTER IV.

SEBASTOPOL—PRIVATE DENIS CORBETT—MOVE TO INKERMAN — PLAGUE OF EGYPT — CHOLERA—FIRST BOMBARDMENT—OCTOBER 25TH—LITTLE INKERMAN—BURYING THE DEAD—BATTLE OF INKERMAN . . . . . . . . 49

## CHAPTER V.

AFTER THE BATTLE—BRITISH AND FRENCH LOSSES—ARRIVAL OF 62ND REGIMENT—GREAT STORM OF 14TH OF NOVEMBER—LOSSES AMONGST SHIPPING—ARRIVAL OF BAGGAGE—DRAFTS FOR 55TH—RAIN AND SNOW—"THE NAILS"—EFFECTS OF A ROUND SHOT—CHRISTMAS DAY—I GO ON BOARD SHIP SICK—END OF 1854 . . . 78

## CHAPTER VI.

COMMENCEMENT OF 1855—FROST AND SNOW—SUFFERINGS OF THE ARMY — STORMS, DEATHS, GAZETTE—RETURN TO CAMP—IMPROVEMENT IN CONDITION OF TROOPS — SUPPLIES—WELBECK ALE—BUSHMILLS WHISKEY—DR. CHILLEY PINE—VISITORS TO INKERMAN—HEAVY SNOWSTORMS—INSPECTIONS. . . . . . . 96

## CHAPTER VII.

INSPECTIONS—DESTRUCTION OF MUSKETRY REDOUBT—NIGHT BEFORE SORTIE—HEDLEY VICARS—MOVE OF 2ND DIVISION—SECOND BOMBARDMENT—NAVAL BRIGADE, ARTILLERY, ENGINEERS—EXPEDITION TO KERTCH—MISS NIGHTINGALE—SOYER—MONASTERY OF ST. GEORGE . . . 111

## CHAPTER VIII.

QUEEN'S BIRTHDAY PARADE—KERTCH TAKEN—ARRIVAL OF CAPTAIN R. HUME AND CAPTAIN CURE—THIRD BOMBARDMENT—ASSAULT ON MAMELON AND QUARRIES—DEATH OF THORLEY STONE—LOSSES OF 55TH—FOUGASSES—TRUCE TO BURY DEAD—ANAPA TAKEN—BOUQUETS—VERTICAL GRAPE—FOURTH BOMBARDMENT . . . . 124

## CHAPTER IX.

18TH OF JUNE—ATTACK ON SEBASTOPOL REPULSED—HEAVY LOSSES—MAGAZINE SAVED BY CAPTAIN R HUME, SERGEANT TILTON, AND THREE MEN OF THE LIGHT COMPANY, 55TH—GARNET WOLSELEY—GENERAL LA MARMORA—DEATH OF LORD RAGLAN—FUNERAL—BAIDAR VALLEY—GENERAL MARKHAM . . . . . . 137

## CHAPTER X.

COOKING—LIVELY NIGHT IN TRENCHES—HEAVY RAIN—GEESE—PICNIC TO BAIDAR VALLEY—ELTON'S BRAVERY—DEATH OF LIEUT. EVANS—ELTON WOUNDED—BATTLE OF TCHERNAYA—CRICKET—SORTIE—SALVOES . . . . 149

## CHAPTER XI.

8TH OF SEPTEMBER—ATTACK ON SEBASTOPOL—FRENCH TAKE MALAKOFF—CAPTAIN R. HUME BLOWN UP—BRITISH ATTACK ON GREAT REDAN—PRIVATES WHELAN AND DUNN, 55TH REGI-

MENT—BRIGADIER-GENERAL WINDHAM—HEAVY LOSSES—RETREAT—I AM WOUNDED—DEATH OF LIEUT.-COLONEL CUDDY—END OF SIEGE  161

## CHAPTER XII.

ARM-SLING WORKĖD BY THE QUEEN—I AM CONVALESCENT—LEAVE FOR ENGLAND—55TH UNTIL END OF CAMPAIGN—LOSSES DURING THE CAMPAIGN—REWARDS—LOSS OF NUMBERS AND CHANGE OF NAME—REMARKS ABOUT 55TH—CONCLUSION . . . . . . . . 175

## ILLUSTRATIONS.

| | | |
|---|---|---|
| MAJOR-GENERAL J. R. HUME | *Frontispiece* | |
| SIR CHARLES WARREN, K.C.B. | *Facing p.* | 4 |
| MAJOR JOHN BAILLIE ROSE | ,, | 9 |
| CARAGOULA (BULGARIA) | ,, | 18 |
| YURKSOKOVA (BULGARIA) | ,, | 21 |
| BOERKASAN (BULGARIA) | ,, | 24 |
| PLAN OF THE ALMA | ,, | 37 |
| SIR JOHN LYSAGHT PENNEFATHER, G.C.B. | ,, | 41 |
| SIR H. C. B. DAUBENEY, G.C.B. | ,, | 63 |
| SIR ROBERT HUME, K.C.B. | ,, | 66 |
| SIR COLLINGWOOD DICKSON, V.C., G.C.B. | ,, | 70 |
| PLAN OF INKERMAN | ,, | 74 |
| 55TH AT INKERMAN | ,, | 76 |
| BREVET-LIEUT.-COLONEL W. H. L. D. CUDDY | ,, | 85 |
| SURGEON ETHELBERT BLAKE | ,, | 87 |
| COLONEL W. H. RICHARDS | ,, | 91 |
| SIR E. B. HAMLEY, R.A., K.C.B., K.C.M.G. | ,, | 105 |
| MAJOR-GENERAL HARKNESS | ,, | 112 |
| LIEUT.-GENERAL H. ROWLANDS, V.C., C.B. | ,, | 116 |
| MONASTERY OF ST. GEORGE | ,, | 123 |
| COLONEL A. CAPEL CURE | ,, | 127 |
| SIR MARK WALKER, V.C., K.C.B. | ,, | 132 |
| LIEUT.-COLONEL SIR GUSTAVUS HUME | ,, | 139 |
| CAPTAIN WALTER HUME | ,, | 146 |
| LIEUT.-COLONEL F. C. ELTON, V.C. | ,, | 153 |
| LIEUT.-COLONEL H. BURKE | ,, | 157 |
| ARM-SLING WORKED BY THE QUEEN | ,, | 176 |
| PART OF RIGHT SIEGE TRAIN | ,, | 180 |

## CHAPTER I.

55TH REGIMENT AT GIBRALTAR — WAR DECLARED — ORDERED TO THE EAST — PREPARATIONS — EMBARKATION — MALTA — DARDANELLES — CONSTANTINOPLE — SCUTARI — GOOD-BYE TO BROWN BESS — PARADES — REVIEWS — CRICKET.

THE 55th (Westmoreland) Regiment was stationed at Gibraltar in February, 1854, when war was declared by France and England against Russia. Colonel Charles Warren, C.B., a fine old soldier, commanded the regiment, which was in capital order after three years on the old Rock. The excitement in the garrison was great, and the mails from England were eagerly looked for. The orders came at last, and the 55th was one of the regiments named to go to the East from Gibraltar. The 30th and 44th were the other two. Officers and men were delighted, as we were expecting to go to the West Indies in the spring. The change of destination was most popular with all ranks.

That fine old Scotch regiment, the 92nd Highlanders, then stationed at Gibraltar, was ordered to give volunteers to the 30th and 55th Regiments. Upwards of 250 of its best men gave in their names: 150 fine soldiers joined the 55th. They did splendid service during the war. One, Private Beach, gained the Victoria Cross at Inkerman. It was a cruel thing, almost, to destroy a fine Scotch regiment with such a historical record as the 92nd had, and it was a long time before it recovered the loss of so many good men. After we received our orders all were very busy preparing for the campaign. The officers got revolvers and practised with them constantly. Medical inspections were frequent, and those men who were found to be unfit for active service were picked out and sent home, much to their sorrow, as all were anxious to go to the war. Sir Robert Gardiner, K.C.B., Royal Artillery, a fine old Peninsula and Waterloo officer, was Governor of Gibraltar during the time the 55th were quartered there. He liked the regiment very much, and was most kind to all, especially to my brother (now Sir Robert Hume, K.C.B.) and me. We were frequently asked to Government House (the Convent), when Macbean and Duff (92nd), Baynes (Royal Engineers), my brother, and I used to sing nigger and other melodies. After the orders to go to the East arrived, Sir Robert and Lady Gardiner did all they could to make our last days at Gibraltar pleasant. The final orders came at last, and the 10th of May was the date named for the embarkation of the 55th. The 44th left some time before, under the command of the Hon. Augustus Spencer (the late General Sir Augustus Spencer, G.C.B.). If their departure had been delayed, the three regiments from Gibraltar would, most likely, have been brigaded together, which would have been most popular with officers and men, and the 2nd Division would have been entirely composed of regiments from the Mediterranean. The 44th went to Gallipoli to the 3rd Division, and had very hard work while there.

The morning of the 10th of May was lovely, when the 55th Regiment, under Colonel Warren, marched to the New Mole for embarkation. All Gibraltar turned out to wish us god-speed, and all were as sorry to say good-bye to the regiment as we were to leave them and the old Rock, where we spent three very happy years. We soon got on board the *Medway*, one of the West India mail steamers, a fine, comfortable, wooden vessel, commanded by Captain Baynton, an exceedingly nice fellow, who did his best for every one. The following officers of the 55th embarked: Colonel Charles Warren, C.B., Major F. A. Whimper, Brevet-Majors Rose, McCaskill, and Cuddy, Captain A. L. Marsh, Lieuts. Werge, R. Hume, Warren (Adjutant), Grigg, Elton, J. R. Hume, Armstrong, Ensign Morgan, Surgeon E. Blake, Assistant-Surgeon Gains, with about six hundred non-commissioned officers and men. After the last farewells we steamed away at 11 a.m. amidst the cheering and with the best wishes of those we left behind. Our voyage to Malta was rather a rough one, and there was the usual amount of sea-sickness at first. As soon as we got our sea legs the voyage was very enjoyable. The band, under Señor De la Vega, our excellent bandmaster, played every evening, weather permitting, when some danced, others read or played games, and some slept. A few Minié rifles had been served out to the regiment for instruction in the use of the new weapon, and practice went on whenever the sea was smooth enough for the men to stand steady. On the 14th of May we passed close to Maritimo, a rocky island south of Sicily, about 2,000 feet above the sea in the highest part. On the morning of the 15th we passed Gozo, steaming into Malta Harbour at 12.30 p.m. All were much struck with the appearance of Malta. The harbour was crowded

MAJOR-GENERAL SIR CHARLES WARREN, K.C.B.
*Commanded 55th Regiment from 1843 to 1855.*

with English and French men-of-war, transports, and other vessels. The various bands playing "God Save the Queen," "Rule Britannia," and "Partant pour la Syrie," mingled with cheering on all sides, made a scene of excitement I shall never forget. Those who could went on shore and saw as many of the sights of Malta as they could in the time—amongst others the beautiful church of St. John, the palace, and armoury. We got a grand view of the island, town, and harbour from the signal station. The streets were crowded with officers, soldiers and sailors, English and French, and natives. Before we left Malta, the *Baalbec*, with a draft of the 55th Regiment, arrived, fourteen officers and about two hundred non-commissioned officers and men, under the command of Major H. C. B. Daubeney, C.B. (now General Sir H. C. B. Daubeney, G.C.B.). They were greeted with loud cheers by their comrades on board the *Medway*. Colonel Fox Strangways, Captain John Adye (now General Sir John Adye, G.C.B.), and Captain Field, R.A., came on board at Malta and went with us to Scutari. We left Malta on the evening of the 15th of May, and had a smooth, pleasant time, seeing many interesting places *en route*— Crete with its snowy mountains, Cape Colonna with its temple, and many other well-known spots.

Shortly after passing Cape Colonna we came up to transport No. 30 with the 17th Lancers on board and took it in tow. We overtook and passed several British and French transports. On the 19th we sighted the entrance to the Dardanelles at about 7.30 a.m. A small vessel with French troops on board signalled to us. Our captain stopped, and we found that there were thirty-two Chasseurs d'Afrique, with thirty horses, on board. They had been forty days from Algiers, and were reduced to two biscuits a man a day, with a very short allowance of water. They were very grateful when we relieved them and took their vessel in tow. The scenery on either side of the Dardanelles is very fine. We saw the Turkish forts as we passed through the Straits, the batteries all ready, we imagined, to give the Russians a warm reception. The *Medway* anchored for about two hours off Gallipoli. We did not land, so could not see much of the place, which looked very uninteresting and uninviting. A few minarets made the town look picturesque. A large force, British and French, were encamped outside the town. We all were very glad to be going on instead of landing at Gallipoli. From the letters written by Dr. Russell, the famous *Times* correspondent, we gathered that Gallipoli was not a paradise. The troops had very hard times when they first landed. We escaped all that, as things were pretty shipshape when we arrived on the scene. We anchored off Scutari about ten o'clock on the morning of the 20th of May. All were charmed with the first sight of Constantinople, with its minarets and domes. Certainly in this instance " distance lent enchantment to the view."

We bid adieu with regret to Colonel Fox Strangways, Adye, and Field, they were so pleasant during the voyage from Malta. Adye was a most amusing, cheery companion. Colonel Strangways was a charming man, a fine old officer, one of the few Waterloo officers with our army. We all looked on a Waterloo officer as belonging to another age; now we look back at the Crimea as they did at Waterloo.

The regiment disembarked on Sunday, the 21st. All were sorry to leave the old *Medway*, where we had been so happy and comfortable. My brother, Lieut. R. Hume, and I got tents and pitched them on a delightful spot overlooking and close to the Bosphorus, with a fine view of Constantinople. We could see the caïques (Turkish gondolas) gliding about, and the vessels arriving and leaving, a bright and busy scene from morning till night. I did not realise at the time, when pitching my tent, that eighteen months would elapse before

I should sleep under a roof. Some of our officers got quarters in the Scutari barracks, which were tenanted already by countless multitudes of fleas, so my brother and I considered ourselves very fortunate to avoid them by living in tents. The barracks and hospital at Scutari were imposing-looking buildings of large extent, well situated on high ground a short distance from the Bosphorus. They were large square masses of building, with a tower at each corner. I visited the hospital, seeing a number of Turkish soldiers in the wards, looking very clean and comfortable. I thought it one of the finest hospitals I had ever seen.

We bathed every morning in the Bosphorus; the water was too cold and the current too swift for bathers to venture far from the shore. While at Scutari, divisions and brigades were formed and brought together. The 2nd Division was commanded by Lieut.-General Sir De Lacy Evans, K.C.B., a Peninsula and Waterloo officer, a fine soldier, who saw much service with the Spanish army in 1836–7. The 1st Brigade, composed of the 30th, 55th, and 95th Regiments, was commanded by Major-General John Lysaght Pennefather, who served under Sir Charles Napier in Scinde, in the 22nd Regiment. He was shot through the body when commanding

BREVET-MAJOR JOHN BAILLIE ROSE.
55th *Regiment, killed at the Battle of the Alma,* 20th *September,* 1854.

a brigade at Meanee: he was a grand fighting general, and was most popular with all ranks; he always had a kind, cheery word for every one in his command. The 2nd Brigade—41st, 47th, and 49th—was commanded by Brigadier-General Adams, a fine, soldier-like man, much liked by every one. All the regiments in the 2nd Division were in splendid order, the men nearly all old soldiers, "ready to go anywhere or do anything." All, with the exception of the 95th, had been quartered for some time in the Mediterranean garrisons. The 95th came straight from England, and when cholera broke out in Bulgaria it suffered much, while the five Mediterranean regiments hardly lost any men, showing that they were acclimatised. During our stay at Scutari, divisions, brigades, and regiments marched out frequently to practise field movements, &c. The three Light Companies of the 1st Brigade were formed together under Brevet-Major John Baillie Rose, 55th, the senior captain. My brother and I were lieutenants of the Light Company. The combined Light Companies used to practise Light Infantry movements, and always covered the manœuvres of the brigade during the field days. The officers of the 55th formed company messes at Scutari. The Light Company mess consisted of Major

Whimper, Brevet-Major Rose, Lieut. R. Hume, and Lieut. J. R. Hume. It was a very cheery institution, and we had many a pleasant party until the battle of the Alma, when Major Rose was killed and Major Whimper dangerously wounded. The Grenadier mess consisted of Major Daubeney, Brevet-Major Cuddy, and Lieut. Elton. There was a little friendly rivalry between the two messes. The early parades were pleasant enough in their way; we saw many lovely sunrises, and the views were beautiful. At one of the division parades our friend, Captain E. B. Hamley, R.A. (now General Sir E. B. Hamley, K.C.B., K.C.M.G.), had his leg broken by a kick from General Adams's horse. He, however, recovered in time to take a distinguished part in the Crimean campaign from the beginning to the end. The first incident that brought home to us that we were at war with Russia was the loss of the *Tiger* steam frigate off Odessa, where she ran aground and all hands were made prisoners.

One day, when my brother and I were digging a trench round our tent, H.R.H. the Duke of Cambridge stopped to talk to us, and was very pleasant—hoping that we were comfortable. On the Queen's birthday Lord Raglan reviewed about 15,000 British troops, a very fine body of men.

The draft of the 55th that we met at Malta arrived: it consisted of the following officers: Major H. C. B. Daubeney, C.B., Brevet-Major Coats, Captains King and Schawe, Lieuts. Brown, Bissett, and Barnston, Ensigns Taylor, Birch, Roxby, Harkness, Twysden, Richards, and Assistant-Surgeon Norris, with two hundred non-commissioned officers and men, completing the regiment up to war strength—thirty officers and over eight hundred non-commissioned officers and privates. Tents were served out and baggage ponies given over to the regiment. Our first parade to pack tents and baggage upon the ponies was very amusing: many loads were soon kicked off, and several ponies were to be seen careering o'er the plain, but on the whole the first attempt was very successful, and we had no great difficulties as soon as men and animals got accustomed to the work. Officers had to provide their own baggage ponies. Major Rose was a first-rate rider and judge of horseflesh; he bought most of the baggage animals for the officers. I got a capital beast—a strawberry roan—for £7 10s.; my only objection to him was that he always tried to eat me when he was tied up. My brother got a capital little white pony, which he called "Bazouk." I brought him to England after the fall of Sebastopol, rode him in Devonshire, and kept him until he died. It was one of our great amusements going over to the horse bazaar in Constantinople, and bargaining with the dealers, who were no better nor worse than some other horse-dealers, who think it quite fair to take you in if they can. The number of long Turkish pipes that were smoked, and cups of coffee drank, before a pony was bought were countless.

The Sultan reviewed the British army on the 31st of May. I am afraid the British soldier did not bless him, as he did not arrive on the ground until 3 p.m.: the troops were paraded for him at 11 a.m. I believe his Majesty was much struck and pleased with the appearance of the men.

On the 3rd of June we said good-bye to old "Brown Bess." I do not think any of us were much affected at the parting, as we had shot with her successor, Miss Minié, and liked her much better. Minié rifles were served out to the regiment, and the officers and men were kept hard at work for some time learning the new rifle drill. We all enjoyed our time at Scutari, seeing all that was to be seen in and about Constantinople—that very interesting, very dirty city—meeting in the streets Jews, Turks, Greeks, Armenians, people of most nations under the sun, in every variety of costume—a bright, lively scene enlivened by the barking of innumerable pariah dogs, who lay about in all directions. One day some of us went to the Valley of Sweet Waters, a very pretty place with fine trees. Groups of Turkish ladies, all veiled, with their children, were scattered about, sitting or lying under the trees, all gaily dressed. We could not judge of the beauty of the ladies, as we could only see their eyes. They were bright enough, and were used freely watching the unusual spectacle of British officers in uniform walking amongst them. We visited all the principal mosques; that of St. Sophia struck us most; it is a very fine building. We saw the outside of the Sultan's palace, built of white marble; we did not go in to see the interior. We often dined with our friends of the 30th—Arthur Conolly, Green, Williamson, and others; they had quarters in barracks. On one occasion they gave us a regular Arabian Nights Entertainment: a lamb stuffed with pistachio nuts was the *pièce de résistance*. We generally finished up with singing: my brother was the principal vocalist in the 2nd Division. I took my first Turkish bath at Scutari, and felt as if I should be rubbed away. It certainly was a very cleansing process, but I do not think I liked it much; I did not try another. I would have liked one after being three weeks in the Crimea, where at first water was much too scarce to be wasted in a bath. We played several cricket matches when at Scutari— one, the members of the Marylebone Club against the Camp. The M.C.C. made 154, Camp 114; only one innings each was played. Captain P. Crawley, Grenadier Guards, bowled well for the M.C.C. He never forgets having bowled my brother on that occasion. The weather became very warm after the 1st of June, but there were frequent thunderstorms, which cooled the air and laid the dust. The nights were cool and pleasant for the dwellers in tents. My brother, Captain Gustavus Hume (late Lieut.-Colonel Sir Gustavus Hume, Lieutenant Her Majesty's Body Guard), gave us a pleasant surprise by walking into our tent on the 7th of June. He had run up from Gallipoli, where his regiment, the 38th, was encamped. He remained with us until we got orders to embark for Varna. Our men were very healthy, and behaved very well during the time we were at Scutari, and there was comparatively little drunkenness or any other crime in the 2nd Division, although there was much to tempt men astray in the bazaars and in the country in the neighbourhood of Scutari.

## CHAPTER II.

EMBARK FOR BULGARIA—VARNA—CARAGOULA—YURK-SOKOVA—GAMES—CHOLERA—KOSLUDSHI—MARCH TO VARNA—EMBARK FOR CRIMEA ON BOARD THE "TIMANDRA"—GREAT FLOTILLA.

THE 1st Division embarked for Bulgaria on the 13th of June, and was followed by the 2nd Division on the 16th and following days. The 55th embarked on the 17th on board the *Andes* steam transport. We took two vessels in tow with our baggage animals on board, leaving Scutari at 6 p.m., after spending nearly a month very pleasantly on the shores of the Bosphorus. We had a great pull in every way over the troops at Gallipoli, as we had not nearly such hard work, and we were well supplied, getting everything we wanted from the bazaars in Constantinople and Scutari.

The evening we started was lovely, and all

enjoyed the beautiful views as we steamed up the Bosphorus. Flocks of *Âmes damnées*, a kind of petrel, skimmed over the waters at a great pace; they never seemed to rest. The French gave them the name. The shores of the Bosphorus were covered with villas, kiosks, beautiful gardens, mosques, and palaces all the way from Constantinople to the forts which commanded the entrance from the Black Sea: the whole made a lovely panorama. The current was very strong against us for the thirteen miles until we got into the Black Sea. There was a gorgeous sunset, and all enjoyed the beautiful scene until darkness hid it from our view. We then had the usual amusements on board ship—band playing, singing, dancing, &c.

The Black Sea behaved very well; it was quite calm all the way to Varna, where we arrived on the night of the 18th of June. We could not see the shore, as it was very dark. The regiment disembarked early on the 19th and marched to the camp ground outside Varna, which struck us as being a wretched place with very few shops. The French, as their usual custom was, had appropriated the best part of the town; they named the streets, and established some cafés and shops where they sold champagne of sorts, and excellent vermouth, which was described on the label as a " cohite and a coholsome wine," a " white and wholesome " being meant.

Our camp was pitched near a shallow lake, where we did our washing and bathing every morning. I believe it contained fish, but we had no means of catching them. During our stay at Varna we met many old friends, naval and military. We knew a number of naval men, and we used to go on board the *Britannia* and *Bellerophon*, where we were always most hospitably entertained by my cousin, R. Oldfield, Greathed, and others whom we knew when the fleet was at Gibraltar.

On the 25th of June Sir De Lacy Evans told the division that the siege of Silistria had been raised, and that the Russians were retreating. A few days after, Captain Butler, 55th, heard of the death of his brother who had fought gallantly during the siege.

On the 29th of June a little excitement was caused by some Greek scoundrels firing at some British officers and men. One soldier was hit in the leg. There were numbers of ruffians about, so we always carried our revolvers in case of meeting them when riding into the country.

There were some good brigade games under the patronage of Major-General Pennefather, and the officers of the 1st Brigade, the 55th, won all the races, while the 30th and 95th divided the honours for jumping. Most of the officers began to grow moustaches and beards. The order allowing them arrived soon after, and I remember General Pennefather saying to my brother and me, when he saw that we had already a respectable growth, " Ah, my boys, you have stolen a march upon your general." The heat in camp was now rather trying, upwards of 96° in our tents. Whenever there was a breeze the dust was a caution. We were all very glad when the order came to move up country. Varna was very uninteresting and becoming unhealthy, and we all thought that a move meant meeting the Russians, but it did not. We had collected a lot of arabas—native carts—to carry our baggage and stores; they were wonderful conveyances drawn by bullocks. A tortoise could have given them start and beaten them, they moved so slowly.

The 2nd Division struck tents at 2.30 a.m. on the 3rd of July and marched about seven miles to a place called Caragoula. The tracks which served for roads were bad, and our progress very slow. The only remarkable feature about our halting-place was a fine clump of trees. Our camp was pitched on low, flat ground. Rain came

CARAGOULA, BULGARIA.

on and we were flooded. We halted at Caragoula for three days. Some of us tried for game, but were unsuccessful. The country about was covered with brushwood; the hills thickly wooded and very pretty, especially when there were openings, which reminded us of English park scenery.

On the 6th of July we left Caragoula and had a very enjoyable march through a pretty country, until we arrived at Yurksokova, our haltingplace. Our camp was pitched on the slope of a hill close to a thick wood. The view from our tents was very fine and extensive; we could see Varna, the Black Sea, and all the shipping in Varna Bay, and the whole of the plain between us and Varna. In a short time our camp looked quite pretty; officers and men erected bowers near their tents. The Light Company mess had a large bower for a dining-room, and we spent many pleasant hours in it reading, writing, drawing, and sometimes sleeping. It was much cooler in the daytime than a tent, as the sun was uncommonly hot. During our stay at Yurksokova we had many visitors from the other divisions and the fleet. All envied us our beautiful, healthy camp ground. We were quite out of reach of the miasma rising from the lake and low ground. The 55th were fortunate enough to have better tents than the rest of the army; the walls were high, and we had much more room in consequence. When we got tents in the Crimea the staff and others took care that we should not get our good tents again, as they wanted them for themselves; and no doubt they were right, as they spent more nights in them than we could have done. My brother Gustavus, and other officers of the 38th, used to ride out from Varna to see us, and we used to ride into Varna to see them, returning laden with supplies for the mess. We always carried our revolvers. I remember on one occasion when riding home from Varna I fired at a lark on the ground about twenty-five yards off; much to my astonishment I shot its head off. Frequent thunderstorms all through July kept us cool, and our men were very healthy. There was very little game to be got near Yurksokova; we got a few partridges and hares. A great beat was organised, and about five hundred men of the 2nd Division beat the woods; the result was one hare killed and another and a fox seen. On the 17th of July the 2nd Brigade had some capital games; the foot-races were very good. Captain Astley, of the Guards (now Sir John Astley, Bart.), a famous runner, ran the winner of the men's hurdle-race. Giving him 10 yards start in 150 yards over

six hurdles, Captain Astley was only just beaten after a capital race. Colonel Warren, Captain Marsh, and Surgeon Blake, 55th, rode to Silistria. They had a most interesting and enjoyable ride, seeing the scenes of the recent siege: they saw the Russians on the opposite side of the Danube.

On the 23rd of July we heard that the dreaded cholera had attacked the Light Division; there were several bad cases and some deaths. The Light and 1st Divisions suffered much, losing many men and some officers during the time they were encamped at Devna and Monastir. The 3rd Division near Varna and some of the cavalry regiments suffered a good deal. Our old friends the 44th escaped with the loss of a few men. The 55th lost one officer, Lieut. Grigg, but no men at Yurksokova. Colonel Lauderdale Maule, A.A.G., a very popular officer, whose tents were pitched close to ours, died of cholera on the 1st of August. The 95th suffered severely, losing many men—I forget the exact number—at Yurksokova and Kosludshi. The 30th and 55th, although they were encamped close to the 95th, lost only a few men in Bulgaria from cholera—a proof, I think, that those regiments were acclimatised by being so long stationed at Gibraltar. The 95th, as I mentioned before, came straight from England.

The 41st, 47th, and 49th—Mediterranean regiments—lost very few men. Everything was done by the officers to amuse the men: sports, cricket, and racing were continually going on; early parades for drill, practising entrenching, making gabions and fascines, and learning to use the new rifle, kept every one well employed. Some of us used to take long walks to the various villages in the neighbourhood, and, if fortunate, we would return to camp laden with eggs, ducks, and fowl—great additions to our mess fare. We saw very few men in the villages except old fellows who were not fit for soldiering; the young men were with the Turkish army. I made a few pen-and-ink sketches of some of the Bulgarian villages which were rather picturesque, the houses thatched and surrounded with wattle fences. One large village, Boerkasan, at the foot of a high hill, was a good subject for a sketch. Barnston and I got twenty-eight eggs, two ducks, and three fowl there. A few words of Turkish with a great many signs and sufficient money generally answered all purposes in bargaining with the Bulgarians. Our camp was supplied with good milk and some vegetables.

We left Yurksokova on the 1st of August, marching, the first day, to Sombey, a small village. The country was very pretty, covered with ripe crops. There were numbers of quail. My brother and two officers of the 30th one day got sixteen brace of quail and some doves. From Sombey we marched to Kosludshi and pitched our camp near a wood. The views over the country towards Schumla were very extensive. We could not see much towards Varna. Rumours began to fly about that the allied army was soon to go to the Crimea to besiege Sebastopol. Poor Major McCaskill, 55th, died of cholera, much regretted by the regiment. A great flight of locusts passed over the camp one day, and on another occasion a large flight of storks. Our band played every evening—a great treat for all in camp. Señor De la Vega, our bandmaster, was an excellent musician, and a good man all round ; he was most attentive and useful to officers and men when they were sick and wounded in hospital at Scutari. He was with the 55th as bandmaster from 1849 until 1879. Captain Hamley, R.A., paid us a visit, almost recovered from the effects of his accident. He told us that cholera was very bad in the fleet, and that the flagship had lost nearly one hundred men.

We marched from Kosludshi on the morning

of the 28th of August, all very glad at the prospect of at last meeting the Russians. When we were at Kosludshi there was a great fire in Varna, on the 10th of August, when a large part of the town was burnt down with a great loss of stores. We should have seen the fire had we remained at Yurksokova. On our way to Varna we halted at Caragoula and Sombey. I was on the sick list and travelled in an araba with Elton, who was also sick: our conveyance was a very rough one, and we were much shaken. I was glad to be able to march the next day, when we arrived at Varna and encamped, as before, outside the town. Our men behaved very well during our stay in Bulgaria, as indeed they did all through the campaign. We were very healthy on the whole, only losing two officers and three men from cholera; while up country there was a good deal of diarrhœa; I suffered from it for a long time. Our sergeant-major, Henry Burke, got his commission at this time; he was made adjutant in the Crimea, and died in 1892 a retired lieut.-colonel. We only remained one day in camp at Varna, and a most disagreeable day it was, blowing a gale; the clouds of dust quite hid our tents; some were blown down.

On Thursday, the 31st of August, the 55th

BOERKASAN—BULGARIAN VILLAGE.

embarked on board the sailing transport *Timandra*. *The Times* correspondent, " Billy Russell," as his many friends call him, wrote the following in one of his very interesting letters to *The Times*: " On Thursday last the 2nd Division embarked in excellent order. Sir De Lacy Evans, his brigadiers, Pennefather and Adams, were on board before nine o'clock. The 1st Brigade—30th, 55th, and 95th Regiments—and the 2nd Brigade—the 41st, 47th, and 49th—constitute a very fine division, which has suffered less from sickness than any other division of our army. They moved with great regularity down to the rude piers, and embarking, regiment after regiment, on board the steamers, were soon on board their respective transports."

We left two officers, Lieuts. Roxby and Taylor, with some men at Varna to look after the baggage animals, &c., as there was not enough transport to take them with us. The regiment was very comfortable on board the *Timandra*. All were glad to leave Varna, which was very unhealthy. Varna Bay was crowded with vessels—men-of-war, English, French, and Turkish, steam and sailing transports, and any amount of small craft—a wonderful sight. A sad accident happened near where we were anchored: a boat containing about forty Zouaves was run down, and thirty were drowned. The poor fellows had no chance; as they were in full marching order, they sank like stones. I met Sir Henry Green, K.C.B., the other day, who told me that he was on board a boat close to where the accident occurred, and helped to rescue those who were saved. Captain Kane, of the Indian army, a very good fellow and a good officer, was attached to the 55th at this time; he remained with us, doing duty with the regiment until after the battle of Inkerman, when he was sent home sick. The Rev. Mr. Wheble, a Roman Catholic chaplain, came on board the *Timandra*, attached to the 2nd Division: he was a charming man in every way; he never spared himself, always doing some act of kindness for officers and men; he was a thoroughly good, Christian gentleman. He died in October, working to the last, deeply regretted by all who knew him. All the time we were on board ship the weather was very fine, the sea quite calm. The nights were lovely, with a bright moon. Everything favoured the great expedition.

On the 5th of September the *Melbourne* took us in tow. As she went rather close to the shore some rounds of blank ammunition were fired from a man-of-war to warn her. No notice being taken, some rounds of shot were fired. One shot passed close to the *Melbourne*. That had the desired effect. She towed us to Baltchick, where we took in a supply of water.

On the 9th of September the great flotilla got under way about 6 a.m. It was a marvellous sight. The *Vulcan* took the *Timandra* and *Rip Van Winkle* in tow. Some of our engineer friends, Bouchier, Baynes, Lovel, and Graves were on board the *Rip*. We had rather a lively time at first, as the *Rip* ran into the *Timandra*; then the two large hawsers broke, and it took some time to repair damages. All these little incidents relieved the monotony of life on board ship. On the same day we passed the Fidonisi Islands. There was a lighthouse on one of them. The fleet anchored in the evening and remained at anchor on Sunday, the 10th. There was divine service on board all the ships at eleven o'clock. The sea was quite smooth, so my brother and I went off in the *Timandra's* lifeboat to try and find my brother Gustavus. We discovered him on board the *Highflyer*, a beautiful frigate in perfect order. Lieut. Armytage, a great friend of my brother's, was one of the officers on board. On our return we passed the transport with the 88th on board, and heard that the regiment had lost ten men from cholera since leaving Varna. On the 11th the order " prepare to weigh " came, and at noon the flotilla started. The smoke from countless steamers quite darkened the sky. During the day officers were to be seen marching up and down the decks with the kits that they were to land with strapped on in various ways. As there was no transport, officers and men had to depend on what they carried themselves when they landed. This included three days' rations of salt pork, biscuit, and rum. I am afraid that some of the junior officers were much amused at seeing the old officers practising for the coming marches. Some of the sailors' songs were very quaint and pretty. The soldiers used to join in the singing when they were helping to work the ship. There was a good deal of excitement on the 12th when we first sighted the Crimea. The coast was flat and uninteresting; no Russian troops were in sight, only a few of the Tartar inhabitants, who must have been rather astonished to see such a fleet drawing near their shores. The men-of-war came up every evening to guard the transports, all anchoring near the shore. General Pennefather came on board to pay us a visit. We were very glad to see our brigadier, he was always so kind and cheery. On the 13th all started about 7 a.m. Keeping quite close to the shore, we could see a good many farmhouses and a few inhabitants. The fleet anchored off Eupatoria, a large, nice-looking town from a distance. The *Caradoc* went in with a flag of truce. We did not hear what the result was, but no doubt it was satisfactory. We all passed a busy evening preparing for the landing next day.

## CHAPTER III.

LANDING AT OLD FORT—FIRST NIGHT IN THE CRIMEA
— MARCH TO THE BULGANAK — MARCH TO THE
ALMA—BATTLE OF THE ALMA—AFTER THE BATTLE
—CHOLERA—BIVOUAC AT THE KATCHA AND BEL-
BEK—THE FAMOUS FLANK MARCH—BALACLAVA.

ON the memorable 14th of September the flotilla started at 3 a.m., anchoring in Kalamita Bay. The French began to land at 9 a.m.; the British at 9.30 a.m. Our sailors worked as only British sailors can, and our regiments were landed rapidly. The sailors took the greatest care of us, and there were no accidents. The sea was fortunately smooth, otherwise the landing would have been very difficult, if not impossible. No enemy appeared to oppose the landing, and all the infantry were on shore at 4 p.m. The 55th and the other regiments of the 2nd Division were marched off into the unknown land about four miles. It was quite dark when we halted; rain came down in torrents. We were told to make ourselves comfortable for the night! What a night that was! I have spent many uncomfortable nights, but that beat all for utter misery. Sleep was quite out of the question. Any one lying down got drenched. The only thing to be done was to walk up and down watching the attempts of the men to light fires from weeds they collected off our bivouac ground. I have often wondered why a few enterprising Cossacks did not come and fire into our picquets. Of course we would have thought that the whole Russian army was attacking us, and as the night was pitch dark, and we knew nothing of the country, no doubt we would have fired into the nearest regiment, and they into us; but the night was evidently too bad for even a Cossack to be out. There were no alarms, and at last daylight appeared, and very welcome it was to the drenched troops. Our first night in the Crimea decided the fate of many poor fellows who otherwise might have lived to meet the Russians. Cholera stuck to the army, and the night of the 14th of September helped to spread the terrible disease. On the 15th the sun shone brightly, and all soon forgot the misery of the previous night. There was a strong breeze blowing on shore, so it was fortunate that most of the troops were landed on the 14th. There was a heavy surf, and several boats were swamped; the landing of horses and guns was much delayed in consequence. The sun soon dried our drenched kit. Mine consisted of great-coat, which, when rolled, contained one pair of regimental black trousers, one pair of socks, and one towel. My haversack carried three days' rations of salt pork, biscuit and rum, brush, comb, &c. We were told that we should soon get the things we left on board ship, but as a matter of fact we did not get them until two months after we landed. I was fortunate enough to get a second shirt at the sale of some poor fellows' effects, so was better off than those who had only one shirt for two months' wear. Our mess rigged up a *tente d'abri* with two blankets. Our second night was quite luxurious: four of us slept in the little tent. There was no rain on the night of the 15th, nor had we any to speak of for three weeks, which was fortunate, as we had no tents for that time, except on the nights of the 16th and 17th of August, when the men would gladly have dispensed with them, as they had to carry them about four miles from the shore and take them back on the 18th—a very heavy fatigue. There was an alarm on the night of the 16th, caused by some French sentries firing on some men they saw, or thought they saw, in their front. We all turned out in the dark as quickly as we could. It was amusing the way we tumbled over one another. We soon turned in again, as there was no enemy. Major Rose and I walked to a village called Tulza, about two miles from camp. We went over a very nice house belonging to some Russian gentleman, and got some good wine and a wash. We bought a sheep for the mess: it gave us some trouble to get to camp, as it strongly objected to leaving its home. Our troops had very strict orders not to loot, but to pay for everything they took. The French, I heard, were not so particular, and I have no doubt we got credit for their plundering. Water-melons were very plentiful and were delicious. The strength of the British army landed in the Crimea was about 26,000 infantry, 1,000 cavalry, and sixty guns; the French, 28,000, and Turks, 7,000, with sixty-eight guns; they had no cavalry at first.

On the 19th of September the allied army marched from their bivouacs at 6 a.m., English on the left, French in the centre, and Turks on the right, next the sea. The day was very hot with a blazing sun; the men suffered much from thirst. We marched about ten miles across a dry, treeless, uninteresting plain, not a drop of water to be got *en route*. It was a very imposing sight to see upwards of 60,000 men, with more than one hundred guns, moving steadily forward. About 6 p.m. we arrived at a small stream, the Bulganak. It was quite impossible to keep the men in the ranks when we got near water, and the stream was soon thick with mud. We passed a village which the Russians had burnt. While we halted the artillery and cavalry were ordered to the front, as a Russian force of about 8,000 men was drawn up on some heights not very far off, and the first brush with the enemy took place. After the artillery on both sides had fired some shots, ours killing a few Russians, and theirs wounding a few of our cavalry, I saw the first wounded man riding back with his foot smashed by a round shot. My friend, Sir Fitzroy Maclean, who was a cornet in the 13th Light Dragoons at the Bulganak, told me that Sergeant Priestley, 13th Light Dragoons, was the man I saw. He held him while the surgeon amputated his leg. Another man of the 13th was also severely wounded. Maude's C Troop of Horse Artillery made some excellent practice. The army bivouacked near the Bulganak for the sake of the water. The light companies of regiments were thrown out as a line of outposts—Major Rose, my brother, and I were on outpost duty. We spent a quiet night on the eve of our first battle. On the morning of the 20th of September the light companies joined their respective regiments soon after daybreak. It was a lovely morning. Marshal St. Arnaud, the French commander-in-chief, with his staff rode along the front of the British line. When opposite the 55th he stopped, and said, " English, to-day you will see the Russians: I hope you will fight well!" A voice from the ranks replied, " Shure you know we will." This is recorded in one of Dr. Russell's letters. There was a good deal of delay before the order to advance was given.

The 2nd Division moved off in lines of quarter columns at deploying distance covered by the light companies of regiments in skirmishing order. The French and Turks on our right prolonged the line of skirmishers to the seashore. The combined armies moved off at ten o'clock: it was a grand and imposing sight. The Russians must have felt rather anxious when they saw from the heights above the Alma about sixty thousand men moving steadily towards their position. During one of the halts Major Rose said to my brother and me, " Boys, have you got your prayer-books? Let us read the 91st Psalm together." We read that beautiful and most appropriate Psalm for those about to be engaged in battle, and we resumed our march feeling that nothing could harm us unless it was God's will that it should be otherwise ordered. During the advance a number of hares were started. We had some difficulty in preventing our men from chasing them. One man, in his excitement, threw his rifle after a hare, quite forgetting that in a short time he would want it to use against the Russians. The day was cloudless and the sun very hot. A few men fell out, but all rejoined before the fighting commenced. Shortly before noon we had a grand view of the Russian army from a ridge, and all felt that we were in for a stiff fight before we could take the place of the enemy on the heights of the Alma. I don't think that there was the slightest doubt in any of our minds as to the result of the attack. Of course we could not help thinking that many would never live to reach the enemy's position. We descended from the ridge into the plain, which did not afford a particle of cover between us and the enemy except near the river Alma, where the walls of the vineyards afforded a temporary shelter; but we had a good deal to go through before they could be reached. The battle of the Alma has been so fully and so well described by Sir Edward Hamley, Kinglake, Dr. Russell, and others, that I merely record what I saw and wrote down at the time and what was told me by Lieut.-Colonel Daubeney, who was major of the right wing of the 55th. It is only a short account of the part taken by the 55th in the battle. The exact time may not be quite correct, but is very nearly so. Major Rose, Lieut. R. Hume, and I were in front with the Light Company extended to cover the advance of the 55th, which deployed into line just before the enemy opened fire on us, which they did about noon. The Russians set fire to the village of Bourliouk, which was in our immediate front, obliging us to take ground to the left in fours, during which time the regiment suffered considerably. Most of us for the first time found ourselves under a hot fire of round shot and shell—a curious and by no means a pleasant experience. There was an involuntary movement amongst the men to cower and crowd together when the first few round shot passed over us, and there were few who did not duck their heads. All, however, soon got accustomed to the sound and saw that there was much more danger in crowding together than in opening out, and the loose order we got into before crossing the river Alma would have delighted the drill reformer of the present day. The Light Company was called in and formed up in its place on the left of the regiment. Poor Schawe, captain of No. 6 Company, next to ours, and three men were killed by the bursting of one of the first shells fired by the enemy. Soon after several other men were killed and wounded, the enemy had the range, and only our being in line prevented great loss. When clear of the village, which was burning fiercely, the order to lie down was given, which we did without any cover, and under the fire of some of the enemy's heaviest batteries, which were throwing shot and shell very thickly. As we were lying down most of the shot passed over us; a few fell into our ranks; a round shot passed through a man who was lying in front of me and close to my brother. One of the guns in the large Russian battery was pointed exactly in my direction. Whenever I saw that gun fired I looked out a bit. I begged Major Whimper to get off his horse, but he would not. A round shot, spent, rolled to his horse's feet. None of our field officers dismounted. Colonel Warren sat like a statue behind the centre of the line, with a single glass to his eye; he never moved when the shot and shell passed close to him. Lieut.-Colonel Daubeney on the right of the line was equally cool and collected. When lying down we could see the French advancing and swarming up the precipitous heights—very hard work, but they were not ex-

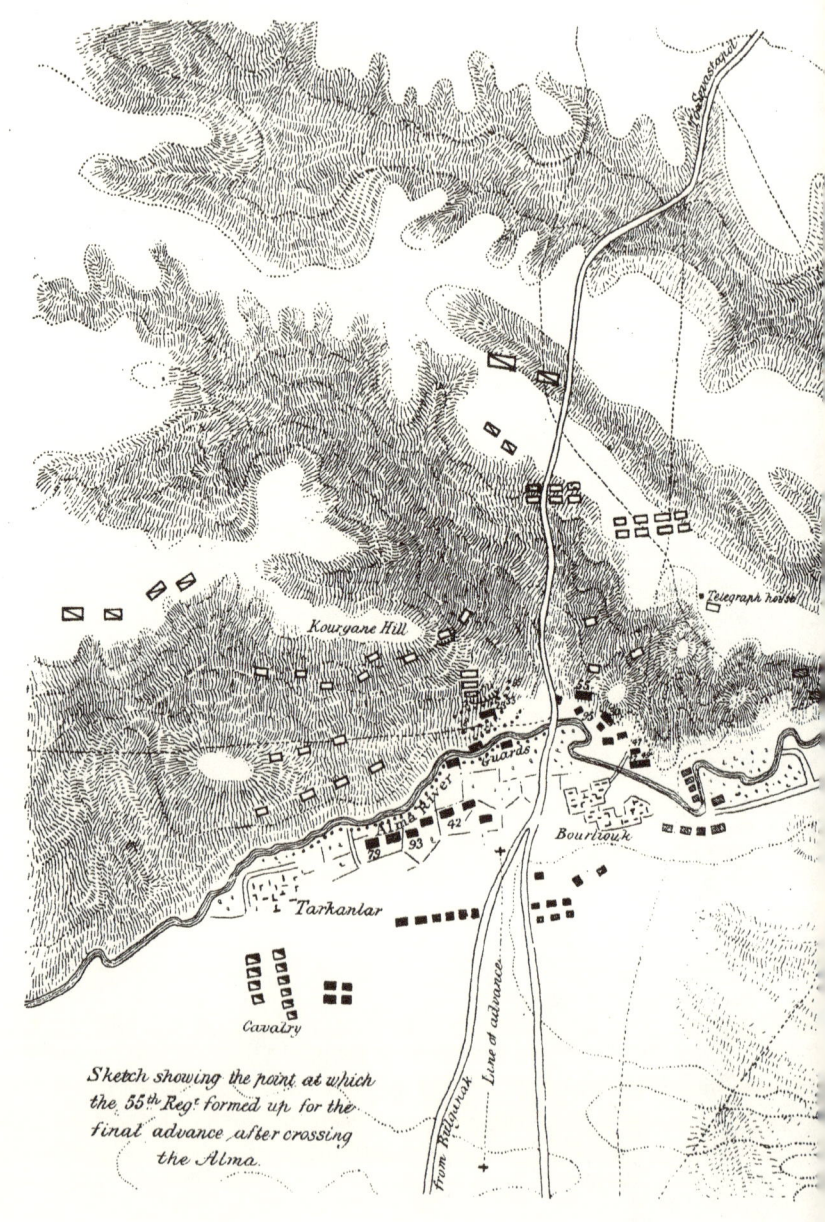

Sketch showing the point at which the 55th Regt. formed up for the final advance after crossing the Alma.

posed to the fire of the batteries as the British troops were. We could see the round shot, after they passed us, ricochetting over the plain, looking like cricket-balls. The 95th Regiment, about two hundred yards in rear of us, suffered very severely —more than we did, as we were more under the batteries: we could see the shot strike the 95th. After lying down some time our artillery came into action—9-pounders against 32 and 18-pounders and 24-pound howitzers. Our guns made splendid practice, but the gunners suffered much. After lying down about an hour we got the order to advance, which we did, getting under the shelter of a low vineyard wall. We lay there a short time, our rifles touching up the Russian columns. We did not lose many men at the wall: Lieut. Armstrong was dangerously wounded there. After leaving the wall we took ground to the right, moving across a road in front of a house which led to the bridge over the Alma. While crossing the road the fire was terrific; the ground was literally swept by grape and other shot. It was near this that our captain, Brevet-Major Rose, was mortally wounded by a grape-shot while gallantly leading his company. Several men were knocked over. I saw poor Rose hit. My brother took his place in command of the Light

Company. We formed up under another wall. While doing so the 7th and 23rd Fusiliers passed on our left, charging grandly up to the large battery. They suffered great loss in officers and men. It was splendid to see them attack. We could also see the Guards and Highlanders advancing up the heights on our left. The Guards lost many officers and men; the Highlanders did not lose so many, as they were more under cover when advancing. The big guns were now silent, the Russians removing them for fear they might be taken. The 55th advanced and crossed the Alma. We fortunately came on a ford; the water only reached our knees. We crossed under a shower of bullets. Major Whimper was dangerously wounded; his leg was broken and his horse killed by the same bullet. The brigade lost all formation while crossing the river, but was rapidly re-formed. There was a slight elevation where the 55th crossed, formed by the *débris* thrown out of a small quarry. Colonel Warren took advantage of it to re-form the regiment. Lieut.-Colonel Daubeney took the officers carrying the colours (Lieuts. Harkness and Richards), placed them a short distance behind the elevation, and called to the officers to form up their men on the colours. This was done at once,

*Maull & Fox, 187a, Piccadilly.*]

GENERAL SIR JOHN LYSAGHT PENNEFATHER, G.C.B.

showing the result of careful training and excellent discipline combined with perfect confidence in their officers, which can only be acquired by long and continued association in the same regiment, and the mutual attachment and *esprit de corps* thereby engendered in all ranks. A company of the 30th, the Light Company under Captain Arthur Conolly, and some of the 95th, separated from their regiments, formed on the left of the 55th, and advanced with it. The brigade led by Major-General Pennefather advanced up the hill towards the enemy's position, a little to the right of their heavy battery, out of which a large column poured to charge down upon us—a very formidable-looking body of men. We poured in a heavy fire on their flank, and two of our guns, which I believe Lord Raglan had got up, sent a few well-directed shot into the column, cutting regular lanes through it. These, with the fire from our rifles, broke up the column, and the Russians turned and retreated. The 55th charged after them led by Colonel Warren. Some men of the regiment crossed bayonets with the enemy, but we could not catch the main body. We harassed them much by our fire until they disappeared over the heights. At one time some one called out that we were firing on the French; the "Cease fire" sounded in consequence. The

French were a long way to our right, and nowhere near our line of fire. The Russians fired a parting shot from the farthest height; the round shot just missed our Grenadier company.

About 3.45 the British troops advanced to the crest of the heights, and at four o'clock the battle of the Alma ended, the allies having carried everything before them. Only two guns were taken, owing to the Russians withdrawing their artillery long before the end of the fight, thereby saving us great loss, while they saved their guns.

All were glad to halt when the heights were crowned, tired after the hard day's work. My brother Gustavus met us—the three brothers untouched. Great congratulations on all sides from those who had escaped the dangers of the day, and sorrow for those who had fallen. Two brothers in the 95th, the Eddingtons, were killed. The 55th had to lament, in addition to Captain Schawe, killed early in the battle, Brevet-Major John Baillie Rose, who was mortally wounded in the vineyards on the north side of the river while in command of the Light Company—an excellent officer, a perfect gentleman, and a universal favourite. He was the head of the Roses of Kilravock, Inverness-shire. His loss was deeply deplored by all who knew him. Major Whimper and Lieut. Armstrong were dangerously wounded, Brevet-Major Coats and Lieut. Bissett severely, and Lieut. and Adjutant Warren slightly wounded. Colonel Warren was contused on the leg, and had his epaulette carried away by a grape-shot, and Brevet-Lieut.-Colonel Cuddy was much bruised by the wind of a round shot, which fortunately did not touch him. One sergeant and seventeen rank and file were killed, five sergeants and eighty-six rank and file wounded. Several of the latter died of their wounds. The battle of the Alma was the *baptême de feu* for most of the officers and men of the 55th. There were no preliminary skirmishes to accustom them to the sound of shot, shell, grape-shot, and bullets. Nothing could exceed the cool and collected bearing of the men of the 2nd Division, armed with a weapon new to them, and with which they were imperfectly acquainted, as there had been so little time since the Minié rifles were issued to train men to the use of them. Had they known more of the powers of the rifle the losses inflicted would have been much greater. As it was, Totleben bears witness to its destructive powers. The British loss at the Alma was about 101 officers and 2,100 men killed and wounded. Many of the French and none of the Turks were engaged. The French lost about 700 killed and wounded. The army bivouacked on the high plateau on the south side of the Alma, near the semaphore, which had been the headquarters of the Russian commander-in-chief during the battle. We had great difficulty in finding a clean field for our bivouac, as the Russians had occupied all the ground about, and the stench was most unpleasant. My brother and I spent a very sad night, as our cheery little mess was broken up, our captain killed, and our major dangerously wounded. Our friend, Captain (now General) Tom Pakenham, 30th Regiment, was twice wounded, slightly and severely.

On the morning after the battle Lieut.-Colonel Daubeney took a large party of our men to bury the dead and collect the wounded that were left on the field—a very melancholy duty. Poor Rose and Schawe were buried in the same grave.

On the 22nd Barnston and I went over the field of battle and saw the different positions occupied by the 55th during the action. Several of the British regiments got rid of their shakos during the fight: all found the forage-cap much more comfortable, so they took the first favourable opportunity to get rid of their full-dress headgear. We came to one place where there was a line of shakos. On looking at the numbers we saw that they belonged to a regiment that only lost one or two men. We found about two hundred wounded Russians collected in one place. We got them some water, for which they appeared grateful. Poor fellows, they were terribly knocked about.

On the 23rd of September the allied army marched from the Alma. All were very glad to get away, as cholera was increasing. We lost three men. Marshal St. Arnaud was taken ill and died soon after. The line of march was strewed with Russian knapsacks and accoutrements of various descriptions. The enemy evidently expected that they would be pursued, so got rid of as much weight as they could. After a very hot march we crossed the river Katcha, and bivouacked on the south side. We got quantities of straw and beautiful grapes from the village and vineyards. The valley of the Katcha was very pretty. The nights were lovely, bright and starlight. Very heavy dews wet us considerably as we lay like warriors taking our rest, with our regimental great-coats around us. We had great difficulty in finding soft stones for pillows, but we managed to sleep well when we got a little hay or straw to lie upon.

On the 24th we marched from the Katcha. During one of the halts our general, Sir De Lacy

Evans, made the 2nd Division a speech, praising the British army in general and the 2nd Division in particular for their conduct at the battle of the Alma. We had a hot, dusty march until we arrived at the river Belbek, running through a beautiful, well-cultivated valley abounding in fruit. Mr. Wheble gave me some fruit, which tasted delicious after the hot, dusty march. We crowned the heights on the south side of the river, bivouacking amongst low, thick brushwood. We got some supplies from the village, always paying for what we took. There were two false alarms during the night. Some kind individual put his foot through my shako, which I had carefully preserved up to the time, not liking to set a bad example by getting rid of it. My brother thought that we should look more uniform in forage-caps, so we hung our full-dress headgear on one of the shrubs. No doubt they now figure as trophies in some Russian or Tartar cottage.

On the 25th of September the army made the famous flank march to the south of Sebastopol. We marched very early, and had a fatiguing morning's work making our way through thick scrub. The ground was rough and rocky. After a time we got into a narrow road which ran through a thick oak forest. The regiment could only move in fours, and we fully expected to be attacked *en route*. Part of the Russian army did pass in front of our column. They thought more of getting out of our way than of attacking us. We came on a number of arabas laden with clothing and meal not far from Mackenzie's Farm. They had been abandoned by the Russians in their hurry to get away. Our men helped themselves to as much meal as they could carry. We caught our first glimpse of Sebastopol through an opening in the wood. The sun was shining on the green domes. The 2nd Division arrived at the bivouac at about 11 p.m., after a very long, tiring day's work. We had been tramping for nearly seventeen hours. On arriving at our halting-place some of us had to go on water fatigue to the river Tchernaya, and it was past midnight before we lay down, quite worn out. Some of the troops did not arrive until 3 or 4 a.m. on the 26th. The great flank march was thought much of at the time; afterwards there were differences of opinion as to whether it was a good move or not. It gave us Balaclava harbour, without which there would have been great difficulty in supplying the wants of the army.

We marched early on the 26th towards Balaclava, moving across the ground which was soon to be made famous by the charge of the Light Brigade. We heard firing in our front, which we found out came from a small fort on the heights above the entrance to Balaclava harbour. The fort surrendered after firing a few rounds. The *Agamemnon* fired some shot and shell at it, and the Rifles and some of the Light Division advanced against the fort. We halted outside, but close to, the village of Balaclava, which looked very pretty with its white cottages surrounded by gardens and vineyards. My brother went foraging for our mess. He got some fruit, vegetables, and hay, and after an exciting chase caught some fowl, paying, of course, for all. The villagers remained in their houses, and were well treated. We had quite a sumptuous repast—a great change from salt pork and biscuit. We turned into our hay beds well contented with our quarters.

On the 27th we moved a short way towards Sebastopol, halting for a couple of days at Kadakoi, where we got quantities of grapes and delicious honey. The division made a reconnaissance towards Sebastopol, returning in the evening. I remained behind in charge of great-coats, &c. I met Lord Lucan and my friends Walter Charteris (92nd) and Winter (17th Lancers). Both were killed at the battle of Balaclava.

## CHAPTER IV.

Sebastopol—Private Denis Corbett—Move to Inkerman — Plague of Egypt — Cholera — First Bombardment—October 25th—Little Inkerman—Burying the Dead—Battle of Inkerman.

ON the 29th of September the 2nd Division moved up to the plateau overlooking Sebastopol. The day was lovely and clear. We had a grand view of Sebastopol, the Russian fleet and batteries. The forts looked formidable; the land defences on the south side did not look much. The Russians were very busy strengthening them and throwing up those earthworks that were to keep us before Sebastopol for many weary months. None of us realised that nearly a year would elapse before the final assault and capture took place. The nights began to get cold, and we found great difficulty in keeping warm with only our regimental great-coats for a covering. Fleas abounded:

they did not add to our comfort. The divisions turned out every morning before daybreak, remaining under arms until there was no chance of an attack. The Russians fired long shots at us, doing little or no damage. Officers and men built small stone shelters to keep off the cutting wind. All began to find the ground very hard, and our bones ached when we got up every morning.

One of the 55th, Private Denis Corbett, was in a house between our lines and Sebastopol looking for what he could pick up, when three Cossacks attacked him. He got hold of a broomstick and beat them off, bringing one of their lances back to the regiment as a trophy. He was given the French war medal for his bravery.

On the 4th of October the 2nd Division moved to Inkerman, at the extreme right of the plateau, and pitched tents, which had just arrived, on a slope from which we could see the greater part of the British position. The ground was thickly covered with oak scrub, and on the slopes there were fine juniper bushes. Water was to be got close to a windmill, about three-quarters of a mile from our camp. For some time we had a very short allowance, barely enough for drinking and cooking, and about a pint a day for washing purposes. My brother, Marsh, Barnston, Twysden, and I slept in the same tent. We had plenty of room, having no kit to take up space. The ground seemed to get harder every night. We used to make holes for our hip-bones to rest in. We were very jolly, and rather enjoyed the little inconveniences inseparable from campaigning. The Russians disturbed us by sending a few 84-pound shot from some guns near the head of the harbour into camp. It amused them, and did us no harm.

At the commencement of the siege the enemy wasted a quantity of ammunition. They would fire a big gun at one or two men: a cocked hat and feathers was a sure draw. As the siege went on the expenditure of ammunition on individuals ceased. At this time we all, from the general of division down to the smallest drummer-boy, began to be troubled with one of the plagues of Egypt—the cause, want of water, and having no change of clothes. The only comfort was that all were equally tormented. Cholera still stuck to the army. The 55th lost three officers and several men. Lieut. Taylor died at Varna. Lieut. Birch, a charming young fellow, died in camp at Inkerman on the 8th of October, and Assistant-Surgeon Norris later on.

On the 6th of October I marched down to Balaclava, about six miles, with a large party of men to bring up ammunition—a very heavy fatigue. We found a very busy scene at the harbour: guns and ammunition, &c., were being landed for the batteries. The harbour was full of large steamers and other craft. I went on board the *Hydaspes*, and got some welcome supplies for our mess. We got back to camp very late and tired out. The 55th had a detachment stationed at Balaclava under Lieut. Richards. Our batteries were getting on slowly but surely, while the Russians were as busy as bees throwing up earthworks and arming them. Every one thought that when we opened fire we should soon knock the Russian defences about their ears. We were mistaken. Lieut. Elton arrived from Scutari with a draft. He was too ill to land with the regiment on the 14th of September. He gave a good account of our wounded. Many officers and men suffered much from diarrhœa, brought on by the want of fresh meat and from exposure. Our rations consisted of salt pork or beef, rice, biscuit, and brown sugar, green coffee, and rum. We supplemented these with what we could get from Balaclava. Not that we got much at first, having to walk twelve miles; and we were our own baggage animals. We had very little spare time, as officers and men were hardly worked on picquets and working parties.

The weather was, on the whole, very fine. Having tents to sleep in was a great advantage, as the nights were very cold. There were occasional alarms, which generally ended in nothing, but they obliged us to get under arms. One day there was great excitement: a merchant-ship drifted rather close to the Russian forts, and got a very warm reception. About five hundred shot were expended on her: very few struck. As soon as night came on one of our steamers went in and towed her out of danger. We heard afterwards that there was no one on board. A good deal of firing went on every day, and there were a good many casualties.

On the 13th of October a large battery for twenty-one guns was completed in the right attack: it was called Gordon's Battery, after Captain Gordon, R.E. (the late Sir William Gordon, K.C.B.), a very gallant officer, who superintended the erection of the battery. The large battery in the left attack was called Chapman's Battery, after Captain Chapman, R.E. (the late Sir Frederick Chapman, G.C.B.), another brave and good officer.

On the 14th of October the picquets on our right were engaged with some Russians. The 55th and 95th were ordered out to reinforce the picquets. On our coming up the enemy retired without giving us a chance of a fight. Some men were wounded on both sides. The Russians fired heavily on the French batteries, killing and wounding several officers and men.

On the 17th of October the first bombardment opened. The batteries of the allies began a heavy fire at 6.30 a.m. The guns on the top of the Malakoff Tower, a strong mass of masonry, were silenced by our artillery in about an hour, but those in the earthworks surrounding the Malakoff kept up their fire all day. We had a capital view of the bombardment from a stone wall to the right of our camp. It was very exciting to watch the effect of our guns, and we were delighted when we saw the guns on the top of the Malakoff dismounted and silenced. Two magazines blew up in the French lines, causing our allies to cease firing early in the day—a serious loss. A small magazine blew up in one of our batteries, doing very little damage. About 2 p.m. the combined fleets commenced their attack on the harbour defences, and kept up a tremendous cannonade until darkness set in. The effect of the ships bombarding and the batteries replying was very grand. Fort Constantine was a good deal knocked about, but no very material damage was done considering the immense quantities of shot and shell that were expended. We could see hundreds of shot fall into the harbour behind the forts. The fleets lost about 46 men killed and 230 wounded. Our batteries were splendidly fought, having to keep up a fire for themselves and the French, who were for the time *hors de combat*. On the 18th the bombardment continued as briskly as ever. The Russians mounted fresh guns during the night in their earthworks to replace those that were disabled on the 17th, except on the Malakoff Tower, which they left as it was. The French repaired damages, and all looked forward to the assault, but alas! all were doomed to disappointment, and visions of having to spend the winter on the bleak plateau dawned upon all.

Two explosions took place in Sebastopol on the 18th. A number of officers and men were killed and wounded during the six days the bombardment lasted.

On the 21st we heard that the Russians had made a sortie on the French; they spiked five French mortars before they were driven back with a loss of fourteen killed and several wounded. The Russians at this time threw up a small work in the ruins of Inkerman, on the north side of the Tchernaya: they sent some shots from it over our camp. We threw up a two-gun battery and soon silenced the opposition. The 1st and 2nd Divisions turned out to cut off a Russian convoy, which was supposed to be going into or leaving Sebastopol. We saw no convoy, so after having some shots fired at us we returned to camp. My brother Gustavus paid us occasional visits, giving us all the news from the left attack.

On the 25th of October I went on outlying picquet. Lieut.-Colonel Daubeney was the field officer. My picquet was on Shell Hill overlooking the head of the harbour. During the day a number of Russians crept up near my sentries, evidently reconnoitring. My men had a good deal of shooting at them. Lieut.-Colonel the Hon. Percy Herbert, Assistant-Quartermaster-General, 2nd Division, came to visit my picquet. He had his cocked hat and feathers on. I knew that the moment the Russians saw him we should have a lively time. So we had. The instant we put in an appearance over the brow of the hill a round shot passed close to us. The colonel and I ducked. He said to me, " We ought not to mind the sound of a round shot after our experience at the Alma." Several other shot followed in quick succession. We then thought that "discretion was the better part of valour," so got under cover. Heavy firing was heard towards Balaclava. In the evening a rumour reached us that a battle had been fought, and that our Light Cavalry Brigade was almost destroyed.

On the morning of the 26th we heard all about the fight of Balaclava. The detachment of the 55th Regiment, under Lieut. Richards, chiefly convalescents, was posted in the gorge of Balaclava, and were on the right of the Highlanders at the time of the Russian cavalry charge on the "thin red line," and helped to repulse the enemy.

I heard on the evening of the 25th that my picquet would not be relieved next morning, but early on the 26th Atcherley (30th) came out, much to my relief, as I did not look forward to more than forty-eight hours on picquet with pleasure. I went with my brother to see the position of the Russian army on the plain of Balaclava. We could not see the scene of the charge; we could see a portion of the Russian army. In the afternoon some of us were looking at Sebastopol from the stone breastwork near our camp, when we heard heavy firing from our picquets. Soon after we saw some Russian artillery come galloping over the crest of the height near Shell Hill, followed by columns of infantry. "Green guns, by Jove!" said Daubeney; and off we ran as hard as we could to camp. (The Russian gun carriages were painted light green.) We found the division turning out, and in a very short time we were ready for any amount of Russians. Our guns, under Lieut.-Colonel Fitzmayer (now Sir James Fitzmayer, K.C.B.), a very distinguished officer, came into action at once. It was splendid to see our gunners at work. One, a red-haired man, was greatly excited, and used very strong language when he found that one of the ammunition boxes could not be opened: he soon knocked the hasp off with a stone.

The 55th was in reserve with the guns; we were close to our camp under the brow of the hill. Most of the shot, shell, and bullets passed over us, so we had very few casualties. Twysden was slightly wounded. The picquets fought gallantly, disputing every inch of ground as they retired on their supports; and in a short time the Russians were repulsed with a loss of about five hundred men killed and wounded. The 2nd Division, the only one engaged, lost twelve killed and about fifty wounded. Captain Bayley and Lieut. Atcherley, 30th Regiment, who relieved me in the morning, were both severely wounded. Lieut. John Conolly, 49th Regiment, was shot through the body while fighting bravely with his picquet. He got the Victoria Cross for his gallantry. The picquets, principally composed of the 30th and 49th Regiments, behaved splendidly; and altogether it was a brilliant affair. It was not talked about very much at the time, as the battle of Balaclava was in everybody's mind. Sir De Lacy Evans and the 2nd Division got much praise for the result of "Little Inkerman," as the sortie of the 26th of October was called.

On the 27th I took a party of our men to collect and bury any dead Russians we could find. We buried one officer and thirty-six men. The officer was a very good-looking young fellow. It was sad to see him and his men lying in one large grave. Upwards of 130 Russians were found dead, and we would see more bodies lying beyond where we went. Nearly all the Russians wore long boots; our men got a number of them, and found them most useful during the winter. The Russians brought entrenching tools with them, evidently intending to establish themselves on our right preparatory to the operations on the 5th of November.

On the night of the 27th there was an alarm in camp caused by a number of horses, belonging to some Russian cavalry regiment, having broken loose. They came galloping into our lines, where they were caught. All were handed over to our commissariat. They were all greys, and appeared to be good, strong, serviceable animals. My brother, who was on picquet, got a nice horse, but had to hand him over with the remainder.

Sir De Lacy Evans at this time was obliged to leave the division owing to illness, and Major-General Pennefather took over the command, and held it until he also was obliged to leave, sick. Officers and men liked him, he was always so cheery, and ready for any amount of fighting. There were no defensive works thrown up on the right of our position, except a small breastwork to the right front of our camp and the small two-gun battery opposite the ruins of Inkerman. I believe that Sir De Lacy Evans recommended strongly that works should be made. A few field works, such as were made later on, and a deep trench cut across the road which led to the head of the harbour, would have been invaluable on the 5th of November—" the stable door was shut after the horse had been stolen." Nothing was done to strengthen our position before the 5th.

Sickness began to increase; the want of fresh meat and vegetables, and the exposure to the cold and damp, with inadequate clothing, began to tell on officers and men. Many died, and others were sent away sick. All were very cheery under the circumstances, and there was very little complaining. Our friend, the Rev. Mr. Wheble, was taken ill and died in a few days, much to the sorrow of all who knew him. He was devoted to his work, never sparing himself, always thinking of others; he was a brave, true-hearted, kind, English, Roman Catholic gentleman.

Up to the 5th of November the 55th had few casualties in the trenches, and the number of officers with the regiment was quite sufficient to make our duties fairly light; but, as will be seen further on, all that was soon changed, and the lucky few who escaped wounds and invaliding had a hard time during the winter. Many applications were made by the commanding officer for officers to be sent out; but nothing was done by the home authorities. There were many officers at home, at the depôt and on sick leave, who were most anxious to come out to share the hardships and dangers of the siege, which went on day and night for more than ten months, in rain, snow, and frost, and latterly in great heat.

We had many pleasant days before the 5th of November. When off duty we visited our friends in the various camps, and at night we met in some friends' tent and had singing. My brother and Barlee, of the Commissariat, were the great vocalists on these occasions.

No one thought that the Russians, after their experience on the 26th of October, would attack us again on the same ground. The 5th of November was a rude awakening from our dream of security. The presence of the two grand dukes with the Russian army no doubt had much to do with the great attack on the allied position, when we were all to be driven into the Black Sea.

On Sunday morning, the memorable 5th of November, the 2nd Division was under arms two hours before daylight, as usual. There was a very thick, damp fog, which made it impossible to see anything beyond a few yards. Four companies of the 55th, commanded by Captain R. Hume, with Lieuts. Barnston and Elton, were sent on outlying picquet. They had great difficulty in making out the position of the old picquets, especially as that of Shell Hill, the most advanced of all, had been changed during the night, and retired from its forward position, on the crest of the hill, to some distance below and behind it on our side, which was unfortunate in its results, for it seems impossible that the preparations of the enemy for their attack on us could have been unnoticed had the picquet remained in its old position. The officer in command of the old picquet, having reported to the officer commanding the reliefs that all was quiet in front, began to retire his men in the usual manner. The old picquets, however, had not been altogether without warning that some movements had been taking place in their front during the night. Sergeant-Major Francis Williams, of the 55th (since deceased as Brevet-Major, 12th Foot), who had gone out about midnight amongst and beyond the outlying picquets, heard unusual noises and movements in the direction of Sebastopol, and was quite certain that he heard the rumbling of heavy waggons or artillery, either caused by supplies entering the city, or by guns coming out towards the Inkerman valley. Thinking it might be the latter, he made a report to the field officer commanding the headquarter picquet. He, not thinking that there was anything unusual going on, did not take much notice of the report, and the sergeant-major returned to camp. Lieut.-Colonel Carpenter, 41st Regiment, was in command of the relieving picquets of the brigade on the morning of the 5th. Captain Hume and Lieut. Elton were sent to the left front; Captain Hume with the Light Company to Shell Hill; Lieut. Barnston with thirty men was sent to the extreme right, overlooking the two-gun battery thrown up by us to silence the Russian battery in the ruins of old Inkerman. The two guns

GENERAL SIR CHARLES B. DAUBENEY, G.C.B.
*Commanded 55th Regiment from 1855 to 1858.*

had been taken out of the battery two or three days before the 5th. The above shows the positions taken up by the 55th picquets, who communicated with the other picquets on their right and left. Meantime, all having been reported quiet in front, the regiments of the 2nd Division returned to their regimental parades, where they piled arms and were dismissed to their daily duties. One-third of the 55th was sent some distance from the camp for water, and one-third for rations, the remainder were dismissed. The other regiments did much the same. Shortly after the regiments had dispersed, some very heavy firing was heard in front. This did not occasion any alarm at first, as it was by no means an unusual occurrence, but being followed by round shot, all doubt was dispelled. Officers and men rushed to their arms and alarm posts, to be in readiness for anything that might happen. Owing to the absence of the men sent for rations and water, the brigades turned out very weak to withstand the first attack. The old picquets, on hearing the attack on those who had just relieved them, returned to their support. The new picquets of the 2nd Brigade, 2nd Division, 41st, 47th, and 49th Regiments, on the left of Captain Hume, were first attacked, and he, being satisfied that his men were of little use behind Shell Hill, immediately moved them forward to the former position on the crest of the hill. At this time the fog was very dense; sometimes nothing could be seen ten yards in front; but on one or two occasions during the day the fog lifted for a few minutes like a curtain, showing the city of Sebastopol and the harbour in bright sunshine. It was during one of these lifts that the picquets saw the columns of Russians marching towards them on the plateau between Shell Hill and Sebastopol. They were advancing in heavy masses of infantry, with artillery on the right of the British position, which was occupied by the 2nd Division, commanded by Major-General Pennefather, in the absence of Sir De Lacy Evans, who was ill on board ship at Balaclava. He came up during the battle, but did not take the command from General Pennefather. This gave the command of the 1st Brigade to Colonel Warren, 55th, and the 55th Regiment to Lieut.-Colonel Daubeney, to whom I am indebted for the greater part of this account of the 55th at Inkerman, he having greater opportunities of seeing what the regiment did than any other officer in the regiment. The picquets did their best to delay the advance of the enemy, and especially of their artillery, but being driven in by superior numbers, they retired slowly towards the ridge occupied by the main body of the 2nd Division. Captain Hume being severely wounded, the command of his picquet devolved upon Lieut. Elton, who had been sent to reinforce Captain Hume's party. A few of our rifles had been loaded for some time, and the powder in the nipples had become so damp that some of the rifles would not go off. Captain Hume, after he was wounded, and before means could be found to move him off the field, occupied himself in removing the nipples of the rifles brought to him, putting in fresh powder and then screwing the nipples on again—a splendid example of coolness and indifference to danger, which encouraged his men to face the fearful odds against them so bravely. It was during the picquet fight that a soldier of the 55th distinguished himself by an act of bravery which procured for him the much-coveted decoration of the Victoria Cross. Private Thomas Beach, of the Grenadier company, one of our volunteers from the 92nd Highlanders, seeing that Lieut.-Colonel Carpenter, 41st Regiment, was lying wounded on the ground, surrounded by five Russian soldiers, who were stabbing him with their bayonets, rushed at them single-handed,

Maull & Fox, 187a, Piccadilly.]

LIEUT.-GENERAL SIR ROBERT HUME, K.C.B.
*Commanded 55th Regiment from 1858 to 1874.*

bayonetted two of them, and drove the others off. The Colonel was thereby rescued from their barbarity, but died shortly after from the wounds he had received.

The portion of the 55th picquet, detached to the two-gun battery on the right, under Lieut. Barnston, had also some very hard fighting; he did not occupy the battery, but a small hill a few paces from it overlooking it, sending six of his men to the end of a spur to the left front of the battery. After he had been in his position about twenty minutes he heard firing in his front, and, being anxious for the safety of his six men, ran down to look after them. To his dismay he found that they had been forced to retire by superior numbers, and the Russians were looting the things they had left behind them. He retired at once to the rest of his men, and, charging down upon the enemy, drove them off for the moment; then, seeing that he was greatly outnumbered, he retired his party slowly, keeping up a heavy fire until he joined the main body of the picquet. It was during this retreat, and while cheering on his men, he saw a Russian officer on a pony leading his men most gallantly. Lieut. Barnston pointed him out to Private Bell, 55th Regiment, who knocked him over with the first shot. Lieut. Barnston was dangerously wounded soon after. During this time all the picquets had been retiring slowly on the main position, inflicting heavy losses on the enemy, especially on their artillery, impeding their advance, which had been very rapid at first, so as to give time for the division to form up and receive the impending attack. Owing to the fog, which rendered all organised movement impossible, every officer felt it incumbent to act on his own responsibility and to the best of his judgment, as circumstances might dictate. The picquets of the various regiments got mixed up, and the men followed any leader, no matter to what regiment he belonged, or joined the first regiment they came across until the battle was ended. Very few of the 55th rejoined their regiment until the end of the day. The 1st Brigade, 2nd Division, 30th, 55th, and 95th Regiments, had originally occupied, as previously stated, their usual alarm posts, but the fog was so thick and the calls for reinforcements to the front so numerous that each regiment, and even each company, was soon left to its own devices, and fought here and there as opportunity offered. The sick, who had been for some time exposed to a heavy fire of shot and shell, were moved to a comparatively safe place near the windmill, where the wounded were brought in great numbers during the battle.

The 55th, or rather so much of it as had not been sent on picquet, amounting to one hundred men, was posted on the extreme left of the ridge, behind a loose stone wall about 4½ feet high and from 25 to 30 feet long. They had orders from Major-General Pennefather to hold it to the last, or if temporarily obliged to leave it to repel an attack, to return and at all hazards to prevent the enemy from occupying it. This wall was hardly bullet proof, but its situation made it of much importance. Some attempt had been made on both sides of the road leading down to the Inkerman valley to throw up some earthworks, behind which some 9-pounder field guns were placed. These works and the stone wall formed the key of the position, and it was to gain possession of them that great efforts were made by a large portion of the Russian army during the day. It was soon felt (for we could not see any distance owing to the fog) that the enemy was in great force in our front. His artillery was very active, and they expended a large quantity of shot and shell on the rear of our position, where they imagined we had large reserves, but where, in reality, there were only a few poor baggage ponies, some of whom were killed. Our artillery was splendidly fought; they suffered greatly in men and horses, and had as much as they could do to hold their own against superior numbers and the heavier metal of the Russian artillery, when one of the great episodes of the battle took place which enabled our artillery to turn the tables on the enemy.

Lieut.-Colonel Collingwood Dickson (now Sir Collingwood Dickson, R.A., V.C., G.C.B.), by great exertions, and in the face of a tremendous fire, brought up two 18-pounder guns to the breastwork on the right of the road, and thereby recovering our superiority over the Russian artillery, and keeping it until the end of the battle. I am much indebted to Sir Collingwood Dickson for the following account of the bringing up of the 18-pounders: "I had only two 18-pounders with me, but as these were of heavier metal and superior calibre to the guns of the Russian field artillery, we were enabled not only to cope with them and to keep down their fire, but to overwhelm them wherever we directed our fire along their lines of batteries, and the superior range of our guns was such that they could not retire to any distance to keep out of the range of the 18-pounders without losing the power of returning our fire, and so we eventually compelled the Russians to withdraw their artillery from the field, and we mauled them terribly in their retreat, besides compelling General

Army & Navy Auxiliary,] [Francis Street, Westminster

GENERAL SIR COLLINGWOOD DICKSON, V.C., G.C.B.
*Royal Artillery.*

Daunenburg, the Russian commander-in-chief, and his staff to make a precipitate retreat from a point over two thousand yards from our guns. Prince Menzikoff was pleased to state in his despatches that the English brought up their siege train against his artillery (accounting thereby in a great measure for the Russian defeat). This would have been impossible, and we had difficulty enough in getting the two guns over one and a half miles from our camp over rough ground and up a steep hill to the scene of action. These guns, with their ammunition carts, &c., were drawn by drag ropes: about 150 men (gunners) were employed in doing this. When we got to the ground we kept the gun detachments with the guns, and sent the rest under cover. We had seventeen non-commissioned officers and men killed and wounded at the guns."

At one time during the day our position was nearly lost owing to some confusion caused by the bugler of a regiment which had got mixed up with the 55th sounding the retreat. Our men got up with the others and retired, giving the enemy an opportunity of getting into the breastwork. The 55th were, however, at once brought back by their officers, and the Russians driven out by a bayonet charge, but not without a stubborn fight. Lieut.-

Colonel Daubeney was engaged with the officer leading the Russians when a soldier of the Rifle Brigade came up, and shouting, "There you are, sir!" ran the officer through with his bayonet. The stone wall was re-occupied, and the 55th were for some time left in undisturbed possession. About this time Lieut.-Colonel Daubeney received a contused wound from a piece of shell, but he was able to remain on the field; his horse had been shot under him previously.

Soon after the enemy made another desperate attempt to drive us from the ridge. A heavy column of five battalions in mass of columns suddenly emerged from the fog in front of the breastwork; their leading regiment had nearly reached the ridge, which at that moment was defended by a French regiment. The rear regiments of the Russian column were beginning to deploy to their right; had they succeeded in doing so our flank would have been turned—a very serious matter. An aide-de-camp rode up with orders from General Pennefather to the 55th, and Lieut.-Colonel Daubeney, having obtained permission from Colonel Warren, commanding the 1st Brigade, took about thirty non-commissioned officers and men, and, passing out at the flank of the breastwork, charged the flank of the 2nd Battalion the Russian column, and he and his men managed to get right through the battalion, destroying its formation. The leading battalion was broken by the French, and the remainder were almost destroyed by the fire from Lieut.-Colonel Dickson's 18-pounder guns, the shot from which mowed great lanes through the mass at a range of less than one hundred yards, and the whole Russian column was driven off with great loss. This was only one of the many fights that were going on all round. Lieut.-Colonel Daubeney's servant, Private Stokes, was taken prisoner, but managed to escape. Sergeant Walker, 55th, a fine, powerful man, distinguished himself greatly in the charge on the Russian column, using the butt end of his rifle with great effect. The 30th and 95th greatly distinguished themselves during the day, suffering severely, as did the 2nd Brigade under General Adams, the 41st, 47th, and 49th. The general was wounded, and died soon after. They were more to the right of the position than the 55th. The brigade of Guards fought splendidly, losing very heavily—fourteen officers were killed; I saw eight officers carried past where I was. The Light Division, under Sir George Brown, who was wounded, fought, as they always did, grandly, losing many officers and men. The 4th Division, under Sir George Cathcart, who was killed, had some desperate hard fighting, and lost heavily when cutting their way through the enemy, who had surrounded them. Lord Raglan was early on the field, and was much exposed; several officers near him were killed and wounded, amongst others poor General Strangways was mortally wounded close to Lord Raglan.

H.R.H. the Duke of Cambridge had some very narrow escapes during the day. Our artillery fought splendidly, although nearly overwhelmed by the superior numbers of the enemy's guns: they lost a number of men and horses. The best general account of the battle of Inkerman I know is that by General Sir E. B. Hamley, K.C.B., K.C.M.G.

Colonel Warren was severely wounded soon after the Russian column retired, when the command of the 1st Brigade devolved upon Lieut.-Colonel Daubeney, and that of the 55th on Captain Marsh, who took the regiment out of action. General Pennefather desired Lieut.-Colonel Daubeney to collect the remains of the 1st Brigade and post them in rear of the two 18-pounder guns so as to defend them if necessary. The day ended in the total defeat of the Russians, and what has been most appropriately called "the soldiers' battle" finished at about 3.30

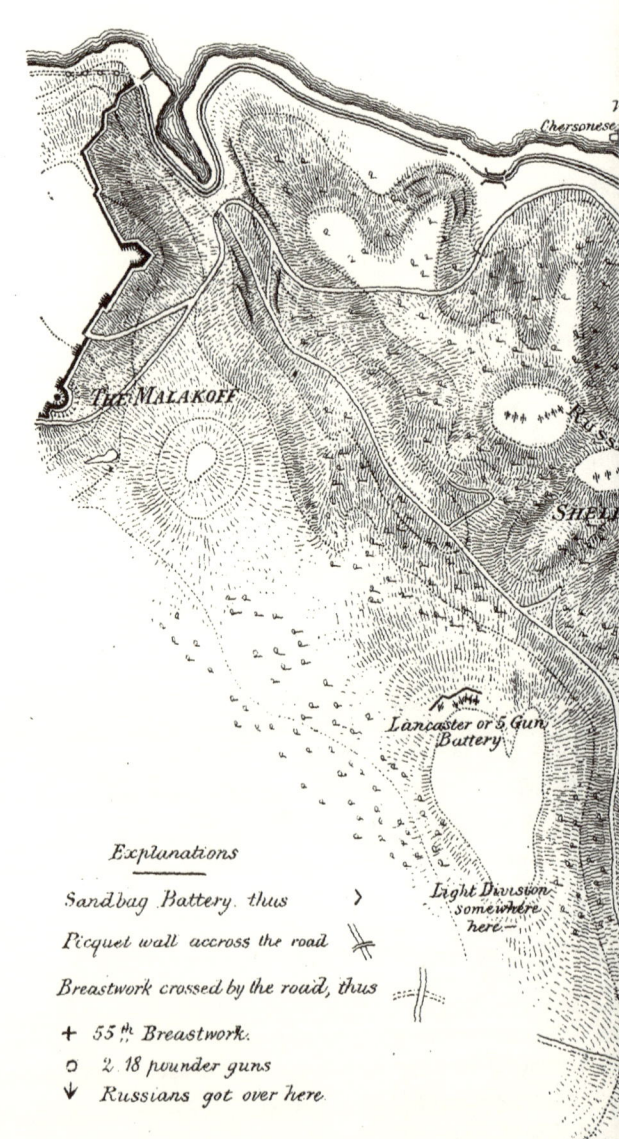

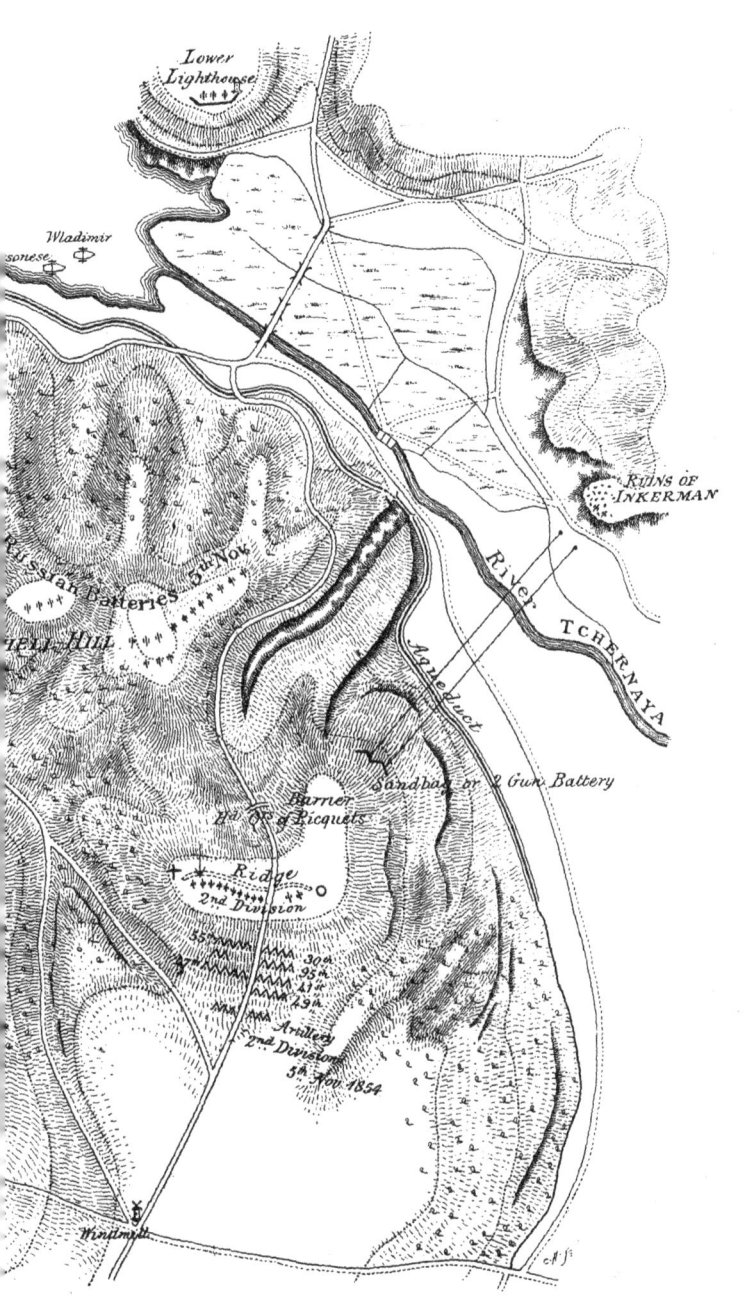

p.m., officers and men having been under arms for nearly eleven hours, nine hours hard fighting, with, in most instances, nothing to eat or drink. Of the 55th Captain Butler was killed; Colonel Warren, Captain R. Hume, and Lieut. Barnston were very severely wounded; Lieut.-Colonel Daubeney and Lieut. Morgan slightly wounded. Six officers and eighty-six non-commissioned officers and men of the 55th were killed, wounded, and missing. About 4.30 p.m. the sick and non-combatants returned to camp and found many of the tents, which had been struck at the commencement of the action, torn by shot and shell. The whole camp was very dismal, dead and wounded lying about in all directions, comrades missing, and those who escaped were sad and weary, notwithstanding the great victory that had been gained against such immense odds.

A field of battle is always a sad sight, generally, when the fight is over, the bivouac, as at the Alma, is some way from the scene of action; whereas after Inkerman our camp was on the actual ground. We could hear the groans of the wounded all through the night. I found a dead artilleryman seated in our stone shelter where we used to sit in fine weather. He had evidently gone there to have a quiet smoke under cover. A round shot or piece of shell took the top of his head off, leaving him sitting up leaning against the wall as if asleep. Two of the occupants of our tent, my brother and Barnston, being severely wounded, did not return to camp. After the fight Lieut.-Colonel Daubeney sent his servant for a bottle of beer; he had got two small casks containing bottled beer and porter a day or two before. The servant found that a round shot had passed through the casks, which were placed end to end. Only one bottle was unbroken. This was a serious loss, as beer was a great luxury at the time. The whole of the band instruments of the 55th were destroyed during the battle; they had always been placed in a tent by themselves for safety. The tents were all struck, by order of General Pennefather, when the battle began. The English artillery galloped over the tents, and all our instruments were smashed—a serious matter for the officers, who had to replace them after the war was over at a cost of upwards of £500. Lieut.-Colonel Daubeney tried to get some compensation, but all his applications were refused by the Government, and the officers had to pay the whole cost of the new instruments out of their own pockets.

Lieut. Morgan was sent during the battle to bring up reserve ammunition, which was distri-

55TH AT INKERMAN.

buted to those men who were found requiring it. The usual plan adopted, when there was a chance of a fight, was for the men to carry extra rounds in their haversacks. Many men replenished their pouches from those of the dead and wounded. I did not hear of many instances of ammunition running short in any of the engagements during the campaign, a good supply being carried by each man whenever fighting was anticipated. Bugler Vickers, 55th Regiment, now retired as captain, distinguished himself during the battle.

## CHAPTER V.

AFTER THE BATTLE — BRITISH AND FRENCH LOSSES — ARRIVAL OF 62ND REGIMENT — GREAT STORM OF 14TH OF NOVEMBER — LOSSES AMONGST SHIPPING — ARRIVAL OF BAGGAGE — DRAFTS FOR 55TH — RAIN AND SNOW — "THE NAILS" — EFFECTS OF A ROUND SHOT — CHRISTMAS DAY — I GO ON BOARD SHIP SICK — END OF 1854.

ON the 6th of November all those who were left found it very sad work collecting the wounded and burying the dead. Most of the wounded were taken into hospital on the 5th, but several were not found until next day; the brushwood was so thick that they were hidden. A large number of Russian wounded were collected together close to our camp. It was sad to see the poor fellows and not be able to do anything for them except give them a little water, for which they thanked us. It was impossible to sleep on the night of the 5th, the groaning of the wounded was so piteous.

Captain Butler was killed by a grape-shot while carrying orders; he was employed on the staff. Colonel Warren had one of his fingers amputated. Captain Hume was shot through the leg just above the knee. Lieut. Barnston was hit in the hip; the bullet was coming out when it struck the face of his watch, smashing it, nearly killing him. We had some great friends killed at Inkerman. Captain Arthur Conolly and Lieut. Ross Lewin, 30th, were mortally wounded. Lieut. Armstrong, adjutant 49th Regiment, was killed. I met his brother, Captain James Armstrong, 49th, who told me of his brother's death. Captain Allix, on Sir De Lacy Evans's staff, was killed, Captain Gubbins wounded, and Colonel Mauleverer, 30th Regiment, Captains Rowlands and Bligh, 41st, severely wounded. We had many other friends killed and wounded. Eight generals of the British army were killed and wounded: Sir G. Cathcart, Goldie, and Strangways were killed; Sir G. Brown, Buller, Bentinck, Torrens, and Adams were wounded. The two latter died of their wounds. The total British loss was about 132 officers and 2,400 non-commissioned officers and privates killed and wounded. A French officer told me that their loss was about 900 officers and men. Sir Edward Hamley puts the Russian loss at about 260 officers and 12,000 men. We thought at the time that it was between 15,000 and 20,000. We collected all the dead we could find and buried them. A large number of Russian dead, hidden in the thick brushwood on the slopes leading down to the valley of the Tchernaya, remained unburied; we saw them some months afterwards—skeletons. We were much struck by the difference between our and the Russian dead. I saw a number of fine Guardsmen lying near the two-gun battery; some, who were killed in the act of charging, had died hard, and the look of determination on their faces I shall never forget. The Russians had a more placid expression.

A few days after the 5th of November I was the only officer of the left wing present with the regiment; all the others had been sent away sick or wounded. As a subaltern I had charge of two companies—not very large ones, as the regiment was reduced to about three hundred men at the time. The Grenadier mess asked me to join them, which I was very glad to do. The mess consisted of our commanding officer, Brevet-Lieut.-Colonel Cuddy (Lieut.-Colonel Daubeney had been sent away sick), Lieut. Elton, Captain Kane, Lieut. Burke, and myself. My brother's servant, Private James Hartley, who remained with me when his master was sent to Scutari wounded, was a capital cook, and cooked for the mess. Elton and I shared a tent for months after Captain Kane was sent home invalided. There was a good deal of rain in November, which made picquet and trench work very trying; it was quite impossible to keep dry, and, having no change of clothes, officers and men suffered a good deal, and sickness increased daily.

On the 13th of November four companies of the 62nd Regiment marched into camp. We all turned out to see the "new soldiers," as the men called them, they looked so smart and clean—a great contrast to the rest of the men of the division, whose uniforms showed what they had gone through. A few weeks assimilated the appearance of the 62nd to the others.

On the 14th of November Elton and I went on picquet to Shell Hill and the Barrier. I was on the latter, which was a small stone breastwork on the road leading down to the head of Sebastopol harbour. The morning was wet and stormy; at seven o'clock it blew a hurricane. I was rather pleased to be on picquet instead of in camp, where nearly all the tents were blown down, and their contents scattered to the winds. It was almost impossible to stand, and often we had to move about on our hands and knees. I got under shelter as much as I could, and sat on a very hard stone. A number of things were blown from camp as far as my picquet; amongst other articles an air-cushion came sailing down. One of my men caught it and gave it to me. I found it a great luxury, as I could not move about much, and the stone was growing harder. My men looked after me well; they collected brushwood and dug up roots, keeping up a good fire during the twenty-four hours we were on duty. My servant, Hartley, with great difficulty brought my breakfast—some capital Irish stew. He gave a dismal account of the state of the camp. All the tents were down, and the sick and others were exposed to the storm and rain. Poor Elton on Shell Hill got no breakfast; his servant, Private Cooper, a Grenadier, was blown down, and Elton's breakfast was lost. To add to our discomfort, a heavy snowstorm came on, and the ground was soon covered with a white mantle. The cold was bitter. My men crept about in advance of our post, looking for dead Russians. They found several who had been killed on the 26th of October or the 5th of November, and brought back several pairs of long-boots, which were of no use to the dead, but invaluable to the living. A great misfortune happened to me. The cold was so great that I did not notice, until too late, that my feet were very close to the fire. One of the toes of my only pair of boots was burnt through. It was very sad, as I could not get another pair for love or money.

We felt quite safe from attack, as we knew the enemy could not face the storm, so we made ourselves as comfortable as we could under the circumstances. The air-cushion was a great comfort. The wind died away before morning, and on our return to camp we found tents pitched and damages generally repaired. Captain Marsh, my last companion in our tent, was sent away sick on the 16th. He had been ill for some time; the storm quite upset him.

In the course of the day we heard of the great losses amongst the shipping on the rocks outside the harbour of Balaclava. Upwards of twenty English vessels were lost; many of them contained stores, clothing, and ammunition for the army. The loss of the *Prince*, a large steamer laden with warm clothing and stores of all kinds, was a great misfortune at a time when they would have been invaluable, and would have helped to save hundreds of lives. Our old friend, the *Rip van Winkle*, with its smart young captain and crew, was dashed to pieces on the rocks, and all were lost. The Duke of Cambridge, who was sick and terribly cut up by the losses of the Guards at Inkerman, had a bad time on board the *Retribution* off Balaclava: he could see all the dreadful scenes, and only just escaped being wrecked himself. Several ships escaped by managing to get through the narrow entrance into Balaclava harbour.

It took some days to repair damages in camp. Fortunately the weather was fine and dry for some time after the storm. Some more companies of the 62nd arrived—a welcome addition to the duty roster. Cholera and other sickness increased.

On the 20th of November the Rifles attacked and took some rifle-pits, losing Captain Tryon killed and seven men killed and about twenty wounded—a very brilliant affair under a very heavy fire.

On the 22nd of November a draft of 160 men under Ensign Johnson joined the 55th from England. About ninety were very young soldiers, who soon knocked up. Several died of cholera and fever, some were sent away invalided, and in three weeks I do not think that ten out of the ninety were left with the regiment. I read the burial service over many of the poor

BREVET-LIEUT.-COLONEL W. H. L. D. CUDDY.
55th Regiment. Killed at the Redan, 8th September, 1855.

fellows, as at the time we had no chaplain with the division; he had been sent away sick. We had great difficulty at the beginning of the winter to get our men, when they felt unwell, to report themselves sick to the doctor until in many instances it was too late. Our commanding officer, Brevet-Lieut.-Colonel Cuddy, with our surgeon, Ethelbert Blake, decided that it was necessary to make it a punishable offence for the men not to report themselves to the doctor when first taken ill. This plan answered admirably; men were taken into hospital for a few days, and then were sent out cured. The consequence was that, when the severe winter ended, the 55th Regiment turned out one of the strongest in the 2nd Division. We found the great advantage of the old regimental system of having medical men belonging to the regiment who knew all the officers and men, and who would and did co-operate in every possible way with the commanding and other officers for the benefit of all ranks, taking a greater interest in them than it would be possible for strangers to do. There were several instances during the siege of limbs being saved by the surgeons and assistant-surgeons knowing the constitutions of officers and men from long and constant observation. I myself am an example.

After I was wounded on the 8th of September at the Redan, the principal medical officers of the 2nd Division, after examining me carefully, agreed that my arm must be taken off. Our assistant-surgeon, Cowan, a clever young Scotch doctor, who had been with us for some time, said, " No ; I know Captain Hume's constitution, having attended him often in sickness. I can save the arm." And so he did, all the senior medical officers giving in to the junior on account of his personal knowledge of my constitution.

We were very fortunate in our medical men. Surgeon Ethelbert Blake was a good fellow in every way—kind, attentive, and clever, much liked by all in the 55th. Assistant-Surgeon Cowan was very clever, and also much liked.

Assistant-Surgeon Fair, who joined us during the siege, was an excellent fellow, very clever and plucky ; he distinguished himself on several occasions in the trenches. Assistant-Surgeon J. Rendell was also a capital man ; he joined us towards the end of the siege, and remained with the regiment for some years after.

On the 27th of November, nearly two months and a half after we landed in the Crimea, some of our baggage arrived, and I slept, for the first time since the 14th of September, off the ground. I

SURGEON ETHELBERT BLAKE.
*55th Regiment.*

did enjoy a real good night's rest on my camp bed. The wet weather and lying on the ground, often in wet clothes, told heavily on the officers, and on the 2nd of December Elton was the only company officer of the 55th available for duty; all the others were on the sick list; two came off in the evening. Lieut. Echalaz and a draft of 130 men joined the regiment—a very welcome addition to our strength.

On the 4th of December there was a sale in camp of the effects of deceased officers. Everything fetched great prices. I forget what a bottle of curaçoa was sold for, but it was a large sum of money. Men did not mind what they gave, they had no other way of spending their pay, and many did not think it worth while saving on the chance of surviving the campaign.

On the 5th more baggage arrived. I got my portmanteau and found a complete change of clothes a great luxury. I immediately buried all the clothing I landed in except my red coat: it was the only cheerful bit of burying I did. My brother sent me a pilot cloth coat from Scutari, in addition to a box of jam and other stores, which were highly appreciated by our mess, and were great additions to our rations of rice, salt pork, or beef, and biscuit. Any change of diet was good.

Whenever any of the officers on the sick list got a little better they would do a few picquet and other duties, then go on the list again for a time. By that means we managed to get through the work without its falling too heavily on individuals. The regiments of the 2nd Division were much better off for fuel during the winter than that portion of the British army on the left of the position. We had any amount of brushwood at first close to our camp. When that was cut down we had the roots to fall back upon. It was difficult at times to get the roots out of the hard ground. Our pickaxes and billhooks were made of bad material, and they broke at once with any hard usage. I did not hear that any of the contractors who supplied our army with bad articles were punished in any way. If a few had been sent out to the Crimea they would have had a lively time. Of course we had the green coffee served out that was written so much about. The men used to roast it in bits of shell, and then grind, or rather bruise it with a small round shot or grape-shot. It was not quite as bad as people made it out at the time, and it had the advantage of being fresh. The men always took their rations cooked to trenches. Taking it all in all, there was very little complaining amongst the men.

There was a little excitement on the 6th of December: two Russian steamers were seen to leave Sebastopol harbour. They got on the flank of the French batteries, and began to enfilade them. The *Sampson*, one of our war steamers, came towards the Russians at a great pace, and soon made them beat a rapid retreat. This was the only occasion on which we saw any of the Russian fleet leave the harbour. The forts covered the steamer's retreat, firing a good many shots at the *Sampson*, but doing no damage. A corporal and five men of the 55th were surprised on picquet and taken prisoners. This was one of the few instances of our men being surprised during the siege.

My brother, Captain Gustavus Hume, 38th Regiment, was at this time made extra A.D.C. to Sir John Campbell, commanding the 4th Division —a capital thing for my brother. I had many pleasant dinners and luncheons with him and Sir John in a very comfortable cave, which was fitted up as a room. It was very dry and warm during the cold weather, and cool in the hot.

On the 16th of December we had very heavy rain: it turned to snow, which lay very thick upon the plateau. We found it very cold in tents: the wind whistled through them, and small snowdrifts used to form on the floors. Those who were on picquet and trenches suffered a good deal. This was really the beginning of winter, and thinking of what was to come did not cheer us much. There were fortunately many Mark Tapleys in the army before Sebastopol who were jolly under any circumstances, and who helped to keep up the spirits of others who were not blessed with such happy temperaments.

We heard of the deaths of many of the sick and wounded who were in Scutari hospital. Lieut. John Warren, adjutant of the 55th, our colonel's son, died of fever on board ship. We were very sorry for him and for his father, who was at the time lying wounded in hospital. The accounts of the remaining sick and wounded were very good. Many officers and men of the 2nd Division were sent away from the front sick; many died before they reached England. The 55th kept up to a good strength, thanks to our commanding officer and surgeon.

The 95th, in our brigade, were very sickly; they lost many men in Bulgaria, and many officers and men at Alma and Inkerman, and each day saw their numbers decrease until they had very few men fit for duty. They had some capital officers and very good fellows, who did all they could to

COLONEL W. H. RICHARDS.
*55th Regiment. Carried Regimental Color at the Alma, 1854.*

cheer up and save their men : Massy, now General Lord Clarina, Carmichael, Alcock, Vialls, and others. Colonel Webber Smith was wounded at the Alma and sent home ; also some of the other senior officers had left. The surgeon of the 95th and the other officers called the small number of men who were left "the Nails," as they said they must be as hard as nails to be left, when so many of their comrades had succumbed.

Most of the regiments had some pet name: the 55th were called the " Reaping Hooks." Lieut. Richards (now colonel retired), who carried the regimental colour at the Alma, brought up his detachment from Balaclava about this time. He had been stationed at Balaclava for upwards of two months. He and I had many days and nights together in the trenches until the fall of Sebastopol. He was a clever fellow, an excellent officer, and a very cheery companion. As soon as we got our ponies we used to ride about a good deal when off duty, visiting our friends in the other divisions. I had many friends in the Naval Brigade, and I often paid my cousin, R. Oldfield, a visit. We were always most hospitably entertained by our naval friends.

I found another cousin in the Artillery, 3rd Division, Lieut. T. Dames: he was a capital draughtsman, and made some very good sketches of Sebastopol and the neighbourhood, which were afterwards published. I also met an old schoolfellow, Captain George Henry, Royal Artillery; his brother Charles, also in the Artillery, had his arm taken off by a round shot when in trenches: he died the other day, a lieut.-general.

Many of my old friends are, I am happy to say, still alive, and whenever we meet we talk over the old Crimean days. It was very hard work for the men, in addition to constant siege duties, having frequently to march down to Balaclava, six miles from our camp, to carry up stores, ammunition, warm clothing, &c. There were very few baggage animals left with regiments, and each day they decreased in number, as it was found impossible to feed the poor beasts. At last all that remained were handed over to the Commissariat, with the exception of a few belonging to the officers. I had "Bazouk" as my charger. The road near Balaclava from Kadakoi to the harbour was a real "Slough of Despond," running through what were beautiful vineyards and orchards when we first saw the place. It was now a sea of mud, with broken-down carts and waggons, dead animals lying about in all directions. As an Irish major said, "It was alive with dead animals." The weary soldiers had to make their way through all this when they were sent on fatigue to Balaclava. Simpson's sketches give a very good idea of the road near Balaclava, his "commissariat difficulties," and Dr. Billy Russell's graphic letters to *The Times* show what those difficulties really were. One of the saddest sights on the road was the number of sick being taken down to be put on board ship, many of the poor fellows only just alive, some actually dying *en route.*

On the 23rd of December I took a party of our men into a new work which had been thrown up to the right of our position at Inkerman. The Russians fired a number of shot and shell at us during the day, making us feel rather uncomfortable as they enfiladed the work. I was behind a traverse when a round shot struck the opposite side, killing two of my men, taking the head off one of the last draft. The poor fellow was laughing at the time. I found the head with a smile still on the face. It was rather a ghastly sight. I often think of that head.

On Christmas Day there was a very hard black frost, with bright sunshine—a very enjoyable day for those who were in good health and off duty. Our mess got a small leg of mutton weighing about four pounds; it cost seven shillings—not very dear considering the scarcity of fresh meat My servant, Hartley, made a capital plum-pudding, and there was a real good Christmas dinner. I was too ill to eat anything, so I lay on a camp bed watching the others enjoying the unwonted good fare. Altogether I had not a very merry Christmas, but I had much to be thankful for when I thought of those who were sick and dying, and of others who were obliged to leave the Crimea, and lose the chance of being present at the siege and capture of Sebastopol. Lieut. Roxby arrived in camp with some of the 55th, who had been left behind at Varna. He was with the regiment to the end of the war. A rumour that there was a chance of peace went through the camp, but nothing came of it, and the end of 1854 found us with an army terribly reduced in numbers, holding a position much too extended for our small force; but no one thought for a moment that any amount of Russians could beat us, even with the assistance of Generals "January and February." I became so ill that Surgeon Blake recommended that I should get sick leave and go on board ship for a change. I got leave from the 29th of December until the 24th of January. I rode down to Balaclava on the morning of the 30th with one of my great friends, Major Patullo, 30th Regiment, a splendid fellow, a good officer, good cricketer, good all round : he kindly looked after me on the road, and helped me to find a ship to take me in. With some trouble I got a cabin on board the sailing transport *Columba*, where there were already several sick officers. There was snow during the night of the 31st, and all found it very cold, but not so bad as it would have been in a tent. All the ship's bells rang in the New Year, making a great din. At first we thought the Russians were coming, the row was so great. We then remembered the occasion, wished one another a " Happy New Year," and so ended the eventful year 1854.

The fall of Sebastopol seemed as far off as ever, while our fine army was reduced to less than 12,000 men to carry on the trench and other duties before Sebastopol. The accounts sent home about the state of our army and the sufferings of the men by *The Times* correspondent, Dr. W. H. Russell, were received with great sympathy and indignation by the English people. Great efforts were made both public and private to send out all kinds of warm clothing and stores for officers and men, which saved many lives, and were much appreciated by all who were left alive to receive them. From Her Gracious Majesty down to her humblest subject, all were deeply touched by the sufferings of the British army in the Crimea.

## CHAPTER VI.

COMMENCEMENT OF 1855—FROST AND SNOW—SUFFERINGS OF THE ARMY—STORMS, DEATHS, GAZETTE—RETURN TO CAMP—IMPROVEMENT IN CONDITION OF TROOPS — SUPPLIES — WELBECK ALE — BUSHMILLS WHISKEY—DR. CHILLEY PINE—VISITORS TO INKERMAN—HEAVY SNOWSTORMS—INSPECTIONS.

THE new year was ushered in by frost and snow and bitter cold. The accounts from the front told how all were suffering; many men were frost-bitten in trenches; things looked as bad as they could, with little prospect of improvement so long as the severe weather lasted. Two officers of the Light Division were smothered in their tents from using charcoal. Hedley Vicars, 97th, was only just saved. Elton, 55th, had a narrow escape from the same fate. He was dragged out of his tent just in time. He was insensible, but the fresh air revived him. Two officers, Captain Burke, 33rd, and Dr. Anderson

41st Regiment, died in the cabins next to mine. It was very sad to hear the poor fellows, and to feel that there was no hope for them. I was pretty bad for some days, and the doctor did not think well of me, but I soon began to get better, thanks to change of air and diet, and a fortunately cheerful temperament, and a "never say die" feeling. It was a great event on board when a pig was killed, and we could give our visitors from the camp a nice bit of pork. My brother Gustavus and many other friends used to ride down from the front to see me and tell me all the news of the camp. As soon as I was well enough to get about we went on board the various ships that were arriving daily, to try and pick up stores and anything we thought would be useful to our friends in the front. I was fortunate enough to get a pair of long boots to replace those that were burnt on the 14th of November. I bought a sheep for our mess, which would have made a capital lantern if a candle had been put inside. It was like what I imagine one of Pharaoh's lean kine must have been before it ate the fat one. Colonel the Hon. Strange Jocelyn, Scots Guards (the present Lord Roden) was on board the *Columba*. I liked him much, he was always very kind to me. Later on, when the brigade of Guards moved down to

Balaclava, he had a tent very picturesquely pitched on the heights above Balaclava, where I used to visit him, and was always most hospitably received. Jocelyn had some wonderful orange brandy, which was always brought out when I appeared.

The 13th of January was a very unpleasant day, blowing, hailing, raining, and snowing. Several vessels broke adrift, and a good deal of damage was done in the crowded harbour. On the night of the 14th snow fell very heavily. In the morning it was about a foot deep on deck. The scene was quite Arctic, and very beautiful. All the ships and their rigging were covered thick with snow, which also covered the heights and country thickly. As we sat by the cabin fire we thought of the poor fellows in the trenches. During the day several bustard flew over the harbour, and we heard popping all over the place. Many were shot, and were capital eating. Our captain shot a number of small birds, and made an excellent stew.

On the 15th of January the augmentation Gazette arrived, and I found myself a captain without purchase, date 29th of December, 1854. I was delighted, as I knew that if I was spared and got well through the campaign I was eligible for, and had a chance of, a brevet, which as a subaltern I could not hope for. My brother Gustavus brought me the welcome news, and we had the only two bottles of champagne in the ship to celebrate the event.

Snow and hard frost continued until the 18th, when a thaw set in; there was another storm, and more smashing amongst the shipping. We had rather a narrow escape of being blown up. A vessel, the *Star of the South*, laden with about nine hundred tons of powder, was moored alongside the *Arabian* steamer, which was anchored next to the *Columba*. The *Arabian* caught fire, but fortunately the fire was extinguished and a great catastrophe averted, as there was enough powder, had it exploded, to have destroyed most of the shipping in the harbour.

On the 24th I said good-bye to the *Columba*, and returned to the front. Our adjutant, Lieut. Burke, brought my pony Bazouk down, and I rode up to camp all the better for my three weeks' sojourn on board the good ship *Columba*, the only time I was absent from my regiment from the 10th of May, 1854, until the 22nd of October, 1855.

I tried hard to become a smoker at this time; I smoked two large cigars on my way to camp; I never liked it, so did not persevere. Most of the officers and men found smoking a great comfort all through the campaign, especially when provisions were scarce and the weather was cold and wet. The smokers had the best of it then, as, give them tobacco, they did not feel the want of other things, and were quite contented. I used to take cold tea and rum to trenches, drinking that instead of smoking. I found things much better at the front on my arrival in camp than when I left at the end of December. Lord Raglan, after the storm of the 14th of November, sent to Constantinople and elsewhere for warm clothing and blankets. When these were issued to the men they were comparatively comfortable. The French had taken over the right of our position, thereby releasing our troops from the duty of guarding that part, giving our men more nights in their tents. The French could well afford to help us, as they were increasing as we were decreasing. With snow and rain alternately, the trenches were nothing but wet ditches, and the mud was a caution. It was not easy to find a dry spot, and our sick list did not decrease in consequence. Men died and were sent away invalided every day, while those who remained fit did their duty without a murmur, a few doing the work of an army. The 2nd Division had a long way to go to trenches from Inkerman, and when the brigade of Guards moved to Balaclava it used to take the trench duties in turn with the Light Division. The usual time from leaving until returning to camp was from thirteen to fourteen hours until the 15th of March, when the trench guards were on nominally for twenty-four hours at a stretch, but seldom got back to camp under twenty-eight to thirty hours. It made a great difference where we were stationed in trenches: if in the advance, there was no rest at night; if in the rear trenches, all, except the sentries, might sleep as much as they could.

As the days began to lengthen the hardships all went through in the months of November, December, and January were almost forgotten. When I say all, I mean those who had the real hard work in trenches and on picquets. Those who had all their nights in camp had discomfort enough, but beyond that were not to be pitied. Warm clothing and stores of every description kept pouring in from various sources, public and private. Our regimental agents, Messrs. Barron and Smith, sent large quantities of things to the 55th, which were highly appreciated. The Crimean and other funds contributed largely. The Duke of Portland sent out innumerable stone jars of delicious old Welbeck ale, each regiment getting its share. We gave it all to our men. I got a glass or two, which tasted like what I could imagine nectar of the gods to be. Our mess got supplies from the ships that were continually arriving in Balaclava harbour. Vegetables came in large quantities from Constantinople, and we were soon able to give very cheery little dinner parties. Lieut.-Colonel Cuddy got a present of a case of splendid old Bushmills whiskey from the north of Ireland; we did enjoy it on the cold nights. Cuddy gave a few bottles to my brother and Sir John Campbell; they liked it much. I think that even a total abstainer, under the circumstances, would have found it hard to refuse a tumbler of Bushmills whiskey punch. A large box of good things came for Lieut.-Colonel Daubeney, which our mess appropriated, knowing how pleased he would be to hear that the things sent out for his comfort added so much to ours.

A great favourite of ours, Dr. Chilley Pine, principal medical officer of the 2nd Division, a delightful, cheery companion, very kind and thoughtful for all, used to dine with us often; he always told the same story whenever he was helped to anything rather largely. "Lady L—— was giving a dinner to her tenants. On helping one of the farmers to rather a plentiful amount of beef, she said, 'I am afraid, Mr. So-and-so, I have given you too large a helping.' The farmer replied, 'Oh, thank you, my lady, I'll stroogle wie it.'" Dr. Pine always said he would "stroogle wie it." Poor fellow! he died very soon after he joined the division, to our great sorrow.

We were often, and for long, without a chaplain. One of the officers would read the service on Sundays to the regiment and bury the dead. It often fell to my lot to do both. Many of us missed much not being able to take the Sacrament. On the 25th of February we heard that 25,000 Russians had been lost in a snowstorm while marching towards the Crimea. The elements, if they sometimes fought against the allies, made up for it by the treatment of our enemies, who lost thousands while marching in the winter to reinforce the garrison of Sebastopol. The Russian Empire was more speedily exhausted by having to keep up the strength of the army in and about Sebastopol than it would have been had the allies taken the place in the first instance and changed the scene of operations to places nearer the sources of the Russian supplies. About this time we heard that my youngest brother, Walter, had been gazetted to the 75th Regiment; he was transferred to the 38th Regiment, and came out to the Crimea at the end of June, when four brothers Hume were together before Sebastopol. Lord Raglan came sometimes to visit our camp. We were always glad to see our commander-in-chief, and we all turned out to cheer him, for, although we did not see him very often, he was very popular with all ranks. All knew how kind he was, and how much he thought of and tried to alleviate the hardships that those who did the hard work of the siege had to encounter. We had many visitors from the other divisions and from the fleet. They came to see the field of Inkerman. I used to take my friends to show them the various places of interest. We used now and then to come across the skeleton of a Russian soldier, killed either on the 26th of October or 5th of November, lying in the bushes on the slopes leading down to the Tchernaya. There were some fine large juniper bushes on the slopes. Many of us got beautiful sticks from them, which were greatly prized. I had one which was well known to the men of the 55th, as I never went to trenches without it. When on the advanced posts I used it pretty freely to keep my men awake. I often heard them say when I was parading my party before going to trenches, "There is no peace for us to-night." They knew, however, that I only used the stick for their benefit, to prevent their being surprised by the Russians. If I did nothing else during the siege, I kept my men

GENERAL SIR EDWARD BRUCE HAMLEY, R.A., K.C.M.G., K.C.B.

awake. I kept that stick until 1862, when I was quartered at Grêve-de-Lecy, in Jersey, when my good subaltern, Morton, took it out, left it on the sands, and the tide carried it away. He was quite as sorry as I was to lose it.

Since I began to copy out these reminiscences my great friend, Sir Edward Hamley, has, I grieve to say, died. He used often to visit me in the Crimea. A great loss to the country and his friends, he was a very distinguished officer in the field, and a very clever writer, scientific and amusing. My friendship with Hamley commenced in 1853, when my brother, Sir Robert, and I were at Granada. We were all quartered at Gibraltar together. Hamley joined our party, and we found him a most delightful companion. He was much senior to me, but he liked me, and we went about a great deal together, when he would point out all the places of interest in and about Granada. He knew everything about the Alhambra and the wars with the Moors, and would tell what took place in such and such a locality so graphically that one could almost imagine he had been present.

The local guides were quite put out when Hamley used to tell us all they knew, and much more. I have always found him the same kind friend during the forty years since we first met.

My brothers, Sir Gustavus and Sir Robert, were also great friends of his. He distinguished himself much in the Crimea, and had some very narrow escapes on several occasions, at the Alma and Inkerman, when his horses were shot under him. His short history of the campaign is one of the best that has been written. He was very fond of fishing, and in late years, whenever I met him in London, he used to say, "Well, Master Jack, have you caught any good trout lately?" He was too honest and outspoken to be a favourite with everybody, but those who knew him well liked him and admired him, and all deplore his loss: the Royal Artillery may well be proud of such an officer.

On the 19th of February the Russians sent a lot of round shot into our camp, knocking over two tents in the 95th lines, but hurting no one. I saw some of the shot bowling along very near a lot of our men, who soon got out of their way. We heard of a fight at Eupatoria, when the Turks beat the Russians, compelling them to retreat.

There was a heavy snowstorm on the 20th of February, a regular blizzard. We had small drifts in our tents; the cold was bitter. I managed to get as far as Captain Layard's hut, and sat by his fire all day; he was in the 38th, and was on the staff of the 2nd Division. I spent a comparatively pleasant day, which was more than those who were on trenches did; they had a real trying time. Colonel Cuddy, who was field officer on the right attack, returned to camp in the evening looking like old Father Christmas, with icicles quite four inches long hanging from his moustaches. A little of the Bushmills whiskey soon thawed him. The snowstorms fortunately seldom lasted more than a day or two; they were generally followed by a spell of fine, bright weather, very enjoyable.

General Pennefather returned from sick leave, taking over the command of the 2nd Division from Major-General Buller, who held it in his absence. All were delighted to see our old general back amongst us, and all cheered him loudly, which pleased him much. Capital short coats, lined with rabbit-skins, were served out to the officers; they were most comfortable, light and warm. Every one was now well clothed, and sickness decreased very much in consequence.

The 2nd Division was turned out at 2 a.m. on the 24th by very heavy firing, caused by the French attacking a battery which the Russians were making. Our allies were repulsed with heavy loss. My brother Gustavus and I rode on the 25th to Balaclava, where we saw the navvies at work on the railway, which was progressing rapidly—a great change for the better from the muddy roads. It was a real pleasure to watch the navvies at work, and to think what a relief to our overworked men the railway would be when finished. We were photographed with our ponies by Fenton.

There was a very heavy snowstorm on the 1st of March; it did not last very long. General Pennefather commenced his inspections of the regiments of the 2nd Division. They all, with the exception of the 95th, turned out very strong and wonderfully clean, considering what their arms and accoutrements had gone through. Sir George Brown was present at one inspection: he expressed himself surprised at the appearance of the men, they looked so well and so clean.

On the 7th of March the news of the death of the Czar reached us, and all began to speculate on the chances of peace. Most were tired of the siege, especially those who went on trenches, and would have been glad to give it up. The 55th was inspected by the general. We turned out nearly six hundred men, one of the strongest regiments in the 2nd Division in men, and the weakest in officers. I think our officers might have been called "the Nails" as well as the men of the 95th. General Pennefather was much pleased with the march past and the appearance of the men, and complimented us highly. Two of the staff, Bellairs, 49th (now Sir W. Bellairs, K.C.M.G.), and Layard, dined with our mess.

On the 8th of March Sir John Campbell and his A.D.C., my brother, paid me a visit. I took them all over Inkerman; they were greatly interested. We went as far as we could beyond our outposts, until some shots were fired at us, when we beat a retreat. We saw a good many skeletons of Russians. There was a very thick fog in the evening when I started as brigade captain on my charger Bazouk to visit the guards. I had great difficulty in finding my way, as Bazouk, after taking me right some part of the way, would gradually turn round, bringing me back to my tent. He did not gain much by that manœuvre, as he had to start again, and eventually we got round all the guards. On another occasion I rode Bazouk to Sir John Campbell's cave; it was the first time the pony had been there. I dined with Sir John and my brother, leaving rather late; it was a very dark night, and the lights in the various camps were very bewildering. I put the reins on Bazouk's neck and did not touch them until I reached my tent, which was about two miles away. Bazouk took me without a mistake, threading his way through the tents of the Light Division and other camps, stopping to drink at the Windmill, and landing me at my tent door without any guidance. He was a clever little beast. I got one or two charming letters from Sir Robert Gardiner, the Governor of Gibraltar; he took the greatest interest in the career of the 55th during the campaign and after until he died, soon after we went to India in 1863. The 41st, 47th, and 49th were inspected, and looked very smart. None turned out as strong as the 55th.

Poor Craigie, Royal Engineers, was killed, hit by a piece of shell. He was a very good fellow and an excellent officer.

## CHAPTER VII.

INSPECTIONS—DESTRUCTION OF MUSKETRY REDOUBT—NIGHT BEFORE SORTIE—HEDLEY VICARS—MOVE OF 2ND DIVISION—SECOND BOMBARDMENT—NAVAL BRIGADE, ARTILLERY, ENGINEERS—EXPEDITION TO KERTCH—MISS NIGHTINGALE—SOYER—MONASTERY OF ST. GEORGE.

ON the 15th of March guards for trenches began to mount for twenty-four hours, but were generally on for nearly thirty hours, from the time of leaving until returning to camp. I have been on for thirty-six hours at a stretch; a long, tiresome time, without much excitement, except at night, when all in the advanced trenches had to be on the alert from dusk until daylight, as we never knew when the Russians might attack. The officers had a particularly hard time, as they could not rest. I frequently had to keep moving all night, from one end of the trench, held by our men, to the other, in order to keep the poor tired soldiers awake. I found my juniper stick very useful on such occasions to stir up the sleepy ones. Poor chaps, they were very weary; but it would not do to allow them to be caught napping. Any man I found asleep was at once put on sentry. Lieut. Harkness, 55th, was very often with me on trenches; he did as much trench work, if not more, than any other subaltern in the regiment, as he was one of the officers who landed on the 14th of September, and remained until the end of the siege, never being absent, and, I believe, hardly ever on the sick list. He carried the Queen's colour at the Alma: he escaped with two very slight wounds, which did not lay him up. He is now retired with the rank of major-general. After the war was over he was transferred to the 5th Fusiliers.

On the 16th of March General Pennefather inspected the 2nd Division, which turned out very strong, looking fit for anything. The men looked smart and wonderfully clean considering all things. I was mounted as senior major of the 55th, my first appearance as a mounted officer. We had so few officers that I was fourth senior as a very junior captain for six months during the siege. The division was put through some simple manœuvres and marched past, much to the general's content.

COLONEL HARKNESS.
*5th Fusiliers.   Carried the Queen's Color, 55th Regiment, at the Battle of the Alma, 1854.*

On the 17th of March, St. Patrick's Day, I was on trenches when our guns made some good practice at a Russian musketry redoubt which was held by a number of sharpshooters, who annoyed us and the French considerably. One or two round shot knocked down one of the faces of the work, when the Russians who were inside bolted out and ran towards the Malakoff. Nearly all got away untouched, although exposed to a heavy fire from the French and our men, who laughed so much at seeing the Russians in their great-coats and long boots streaming out of the work like so many bees, that they could not take proper aim. I do not really think that they tried to hit the poor fellows running for their lives. A few were knocked over.

On the 21st of March I started for trenches with one subaltern, Lieut. Scott, and 270 men of the 55th, to occupy, for the first time, a long line of trench which had been made to communicate with the French works on our right. The trench was not nearly completed, and it afforded very little cover. A large proportion of my men worked all night, while the remainder guarded them. We fully expected the Russians to attack us during the night, as they crept up close to us several times and fired volleys at us. Fortunately they fired high in the darkness, so we had very few casualties. It was a very unpleasant night. Scott was taken ill, and was obliged to return to camp. I went to the French and found their trenches full of men, while we could only provide men enough to guard our trench with an interval between every two men. Notwithstanding their great superiority of numbers the French officers begged me to bring some of my men to support them in the event of an attack. It was very flattering to us, and showed what our allies thought of the fighting qualities of the British soldier. At last the night ended without an attack, and we were very glad to move at daylight to a quiet, safe place. We returned at dark on the night of the 22nd, and my men worked hard until relieved by some of the Light Division at 8 p.m. Parties from three regiments relieved the 55th. One party of the 97th was commanded by Captain Hedley Vicars. I had known him for some time, and liked him much. He was a brave soldier, and a religious, good man. I gave him all the information I could, telling him what an unpleasant post he had to guard. I then marched my men home, very glad to get safely back to camp. About two hours after I was relieved the Russians made a great sortie on our and the French trenches. Hedley Vicars, 97th, and Captain Browne, 7th Fusiliers, two of the officers who relieved me, were killed. After a hard fight the Russians were driven back to their works with heavy loss. Our loss was about sixty officers and men killed and wounded. The French lost about fifteen officers killed and wounded, and between three and four hundred men. An Albanian tried to blow up one of our magazines. He was killed close to the entrance to the magazine. Colonel Kelly, 34th, and Captain Montague, R.E., were taken prisoners.

The French made rather a feeble attack on some rifle-pits on the morning of the 22nd. They never reached them, retiring after losing a few men. General Eyre, who was looking from where I was posted, called the attack "child's play."

My brother Gustavus bought me a very pretty grey barb for £18, a delightful pony to ride, about fourteen hands, very quiet and shapely. Some one brought him to England. I saw him one day in Devonshire.

On the 27th of March the 2nd Division began to move to the left to a new encamping ground near the 4th Division, and on the 3rd of April all had left our old position at Inkerman. We were all sorry to leave the place, which was beginning to look very pretty, and wild flowers were springing up all over the battle-field of Inkerman. Our new position was much nearer the trenches, but was very bare, not nearly so pleasant for a camp as our old ground at Inkerman. We used to have some of our great friends in the 2nd Division to dine with us occasionally: Captain Hugh Rowlands, 41st Regiment (now Lieut.-General Hugh Rowlands, V.C., C.B.), a fine, dashing soldier, who distinguished himself at Inkerman and on several other occasions during the campaign, getting the Victoria Cross. He and Captain Allan (now Major-General), another distinguished 41st officer, often came to see us. About this time there were several race meetings, where we met all our friends. At the Light Division Races on the 7th of April my brother and I were standing at one of the jumps when Thomas, R.H.A., and Shiffner, 54th, collided, coming to great grief. Both were picked up insensible, but soon recovered. Shiffner was killed later on during the siege. I often meet General Thomas at Lord's, and remind him of the racing incident. Captain Werge, acting-paymaster, 55th Regiment, a good flat race rider, won one of the races open to the army.

On the 9th of April the second bombardment began. The morning was very wet and stormy, with a thick mist. Several of our tents were blown down, mine amongst the number. I took advan-

LIEUT. GENERAL HUGH ROWLANDS, V.C., C.B.

tage of our commanding officer being on trenches to occupy his tent and bed. The firing was very heavy all day; several men were killed and wounded. The Naval Brigade suffered much. They exposed themselves a good deal. Whenever they gave the Ruskies a broadside they would jump upon the parapet to see the result, and many got hit in consequence. They were splendid fellows, and always cheery under the most trying circumstances. They used very strong language at times, but did not mean anything by it. It was rather startling to hear their expressions when one of their comrades was blown to pieces, and they announced the discovery of an arm, leg, or other part of the body; at the same time they felt his death much.

On the 12th I took 250 of our men into trenches. We were in the advance, and had a fairly quiet night—only a few shells now and then to keep us awake. Our men fired a good deal at the Redan to prevent the Russians repairing damages. The bombardment continued on the 13th. We were posted in the parallel in front of Gordon's battery. The firing on both sides was very heavy; the enemy's practice was not good. It was rather trying to the nerves of any who were new to the trenches to be sent down during a bombardment and to hear shot and shell passing close overhead; the noise was deafening. Shells burst all over the place, and the fragments flew about, making a humming noise as they flew through the air. It was marvellous how few men were hit during the day; many had very narrow escapes. Our great admiration was the way the Royal Artillery and Engineers behaved during a bombardment and at all other times. It was a fine sight to watch the cool way the gunners fought their guns. The Engineers repaired embrasures and parapets under the heaviest fire, quite regardless of the missiles that were flying thickly about them. They had many killed and wounded in all the bombardments. It would be impossible to find four grander examples of cool pluck than that shown by our sailors, gunners, engineers, and infantry during the siege. The Russians made a sortie on the French on the left; the firing was very heavy for some time, when the French drove the enemy back to their works, both sides losing a good many officers and men. A new chaplain, the Rev. Mr. Butler, a brother of the hero of Silistria and of Captain Butler, 55th, who was killed at Inkerman, was posted to the 2nd Division. He was a very nice young fellow; we all liked him, and were very glad to have a chaplain to administer the Sacrament to those who wished to receive it, and also to conduct the services on Sundays, visit the sick, and bury the dead.

On the 20th of April two rifle-pits were taken. The 77th, with some of the 33rd and other regiments, under Colonel Egerton, attacked and carried the pits. The Russians tried hard to retake them, but were driven off with great loss. Colonel Egerton was mortally wounded; Trevor, 55th, was shot through the elbow; Baynes, Royal Engineers, a charming fellow, one of our Gibraltar garrison, was shot through the lungs, and died soon after. He was an excellent officer, and a great loss to the corps; we all felt his loss very much. The second bombardment, like the first, was very disappointing: no assault took place, and things remained much as they were, except that each side was so much weaker in men and material. The Russian loss was very heavy. The fall of Sebastopol seemed as far off as ever. There was rather a sameness in the work we had to do; one day in trenches was very like another—a few men killed and wounded, and a great deal of ammunition was expended. The French lost more men than we did, as their works were more extended than ours, and were nearer the Russian works, and they had many more men to guard their trenches, in proportion, than we had.

I have not recorded many of the trench duties I was on, only those when anything unusual occurred.

On the 4th of May an expedition left for Kertch. I rode into Balaclava to see it start, and afterwards lunched with Colonel Jocelyn, and had some of the wonderful orange brandy. The view from his tent was very extensive : we looked down on the decks of all the ships lying in Balaclava harbour, and could see all over the country between Balaclava and the Mackenzie heights.

On the 5th of May Lieut. Thorley Stone, a very nice young fellow, joined the 55th, a bright, cheery boy, a good rider, full of life and enthusiasm, a great favourite of all who knew him. If he had been spared he would have made a first-rate officer. On the night of the 5th the Russians made a sortie on the right attack; they were soon driven back. Our loss, one officer and thirty men killed and wounded. Lieut.-Colonel Cuddy was the field officer ; he returned to camp with two bullet holes in his coat—a near shave.

On the 6th of May the Bishop of Gibraltar visited our camp. He preached an admirable sermon, and administered the Sacrament to a good number. On the 8th Miss Nightingale visited our camp and hospital. Every one turned out to see her, as all had heard of her good work in the Scutari hospital. Mr. Alexis Soyer, the famous French cook, came at the same time, and gave our men a lesson in cooking, showing them how to make the most of their rations. He certainly did make some most appetising dishes, but one lesson was not enough, and I do not remember that there was much improvement in the cooking in consequence.

On the night of the 9th the Russians made a sortie; casualties on our side between thirty and forty. The enemy never gained much by their sorties; they killed and wounded a few of our men, and lost a good number themselves.

The 10th of May—one year since we embarked at Gibraltar: an eventful year to most of us. Very sad to think of the great number of officers and men of the 55th who were killed in action and died of disease of those who embarked on board the *Medway* full of life and hope.

On the 11th I went on trenches. Many shots were fired at us on our way down. The Russians knew the time the reliefs were marched down, and annoyed us as much as they could. A sortie was attempted, but we were prepared, and opened such a fire on the enemy that they never reached our trenches. As soon as they got back to their works they opened a tremendous fire of shot and shell from all their batteries. It was very pretty to watch the howitzer shells after they passed us, a train of sparks in their wake. We did not mind them once they passed us, as when they burst all the pieces went forward. The mortar shells, especially the 13-inch, were much more dangerous; they frequently burst up in the air, when the fragments would come down amongst us, or they pitched and burst, when the pieces came back often as much as two hundred yards. One of the 13-inch shells—" whistling Dicks " the men called them, from the sound they made going through the air—burst quite two hundred yards in rear of where my men were lying in a safe (?) place. A piece of the shell, as large as a soup plate, came back and took the top off the head of one of my men. A sergeant asked me if he should send for a doctor, but when I looked at the poor fellow I saw that he was past human aid. We had about twenty casualties on that occasion in the right attack. There was very heavy rain in the night, and the trenches were very wet and muddy all next day. The duties at this time were very heavy. I find by my diary that I went on trenches on the 10th for about thirty hours, and again on the 12th—only one night in bed; this was exceptional. The average for our officers was two trench guards a week. As

MONASTERY OF ST. GEORGE, CRIMEA.

the summer drew near we used, when off duty, to make very pleasant excursions on horseback. The monastery of St. George was a very favourite resort. It was very strikingly and prettily situated on the cliffs overhanging the Black Sea between Sebastopol and Balaclava. There were terraces overlooking the sea, and paths winding down to the shore. Some monks remained at the monastery; they held services in the small Greek chapel, at the end of the upper terrace, for the benefit of those inhabitants who did not desert the place. The chapel, with its pretty dome, was one of the features of the place. We spent many happy days at the monastery; it was such a peaceful contrast to our every-day life at the front, within sight and sound of siege and siege guns.

## CHAPTER VIII.

Queen's Birthday Parade—Kertch Taken—Arrival of Captain R. Hume and Captain Cure—Third Bombardment—Assault on Mamelon and Quarries—Death of Thorley Stone—Losses of 55th—Fougasses—Truce to Bury Dead—Anapa Taken — Bouquets — Vertical Grape—Fourth Bombardment.

ON the 24th of May, Her Most Gracious Majesty's birthday, Lord Raglan held a review of cavalry and horse artillery. The other artillery and the infantry were otherwise employed. The cavalry looked very well considering the hardships their horses had gone through during the winter. The horse artillery looked, as it always does, splendid, ready for anything. I rode with Elton to see some of our many friends in the 3rd and 4th Divisions, and, according to an entry in my diary, we drank Her Gracious Majesty's health many times.

On the 25th Surgeon Blake, Thorley Stone, and I rode over to Kamisch, the French port. It was our first visit to that place. We found it a very lively town. The French had established all kinds of shops, cafés, &c. We got coffee, vermouth, and strawberries at a nice clean café. On our way home we were skylarking over some small stone walls when Stone got a great cropper over a wall which his horse did not quite clear. He was not much hurt, but considerably shaken.

On the 27th news came in that Kertch had been taken with no loss on our side. A foundry and fifty large guns were destroyed, besides a great quantity of stores and grain—a great loss to the Russians.

On the 29th of May my brother, Captain R. Hume, arrived from England. I was delighted to see him again; we had been always together until he was wounded. He, Colonel Warren, and Lieut. Bissett were the only officers of the 55th out of all who were sent home sick and wounded who rejoined the 55th before the fall of Sebastopol. Further accounts of the Kertch expedition arrived telling us that one hundred guns, four gunboats, and about £30,000 worth of corn had been taken, and that Arabat had been destroyed.

On the 1st of June Cuddy, my brother, Elton,

and I rode to the monastery of St. George. We heard service in the chapel, which was rather like a Roman Catholic place of worship.

On the 3rd of June my great friend, Captain Capel Cure, arrived from the depôt. He was a very welcome addition to our mess, which now consisted of Lieut.-Colonel Cuddy, Captains Cure, R. Hume, Elton, J. R. Hume, Lieuts. Burke and Thorley Stone.

On the 4th of June my brother Gustavus started with Sir John Campbell for Kertch—a pleasant change for them. On the 5th of June my brother and I went on trenches. We had a comparatively quiet time until we moved in the morning to the right of Gordon's battery. At about 3 p.m. all our batteries opened fire. The Mamelon was the only Russian battery that replied at once; the others evidently did not expect us to commence a bombardment. In the evening Captain Mortimer Adye, Royal Artillery, passed us, looking like a black man. Some powder with which some gunners were filling a shell was exploded by one of the Russian shells, and Adye was severely burnt. We did not know him until he spoke to us. We gave him something to drink: he soon recovered, and was not marked a bit. The days were now very warm, the nights cool and pleasant. All quite

BREVET-LIEUT.-COLONEL A. CAPEL CURE.
55th Regiment.

forgot what we went through during the winter. Every one was very cheery. All wished for the assault to put an end to the constant weary trench work. The nearer we got to the Russian works the more casualties we had. The lists of killed and wounded grew longer.

On the 7th of June the bombardment was very heavy. Five officers—Captains Capel Cure and Elton, Lieuts. Williams, Stone, and Scott—with two hundred men of the 55th, were ordered down to the right attack with entrenching tools to be ready to connect the Quarry works which the British troops were to storm from our advanced parallel when the French assaulted the Mamelon. At about 6.30 p m. the attack began. All who could get away from the various camps looked on from Cathcart's hill. I had a grand view of the whole of the attack, English and French. It was a very fine and exciting sight to watch the two attacks. The French rushed up to the Mamelon, and swarming over the parapets soon drove the Russians out. They then pressed on towards the Malakoff to attack that formidable work. That was not part of the programme. The Russians drove the French back to the Mamelon, entering that work with them and retaking it. The French, being reinforced, again attacked and retook the Mamelon, and this time they held it. There were very heavy losses on both sides. The Naval Brigade battery assisted the French greatly. As soon as the French attacked, the signal was given to our troops, and they went in at the Quarries. The party of the 55th under Captain Cure was, from being a working party, somehow changed into part of the stormers, Captain Browne, the engineer in charge of the working parties, consenting. The Quarries were soon taken, but not without considerable loss, and our men established themselves in the Russian works. During the night the enemy made several determined attacks on our men, trying to drive us out, but they did not succeed. The 55th and the other regiments engaged suffered severely while repelling the attacks. Poor Thorley Stone was killed while gallantly leading a party of the 55th to repel an attack. He only spoke a few words after he was shot, leaving his revolver to Lieut.-Colonel Cuddy. Lieut. Scott was wounded. Captain Elton and twenty men of the 55th were in advance of the Quarries, between them and the Redan. They remained there all night, repulsing several attacks. Ten men, out of the twenty with Captain Elton, were killed. They were reported missing in the morning. Their bodies were found together when the truce for burying the dead took place. Captain Cure directed all the 55th movements. Colonel Shirley, 88th, was the acting general in the trenches during the attack. Colonel Campbell, 90th Regiment, commanded the attacking party. The British lost about seven hundred, the French upwards of five thousand, and the Russians about five thousand killed and wounded.

The 55th had one officer and twenty-one men killed, and one officer and thirty-one non-commissioned officers and men wounded: a total of 54 out of 205 engaged—a large proportion. The 34th had one officer and ten men killed, and four officers and thirty-six men wounded and missing, making a total of fifty-one officers and men killed and wounded. It is curious that the losses of the two regiments, 34th and 55th, which have since been amalgamated, should have been nearly the same. Some men were blown up by the explosion of fougasses which the Russians had laid down all about the ground outside their works. These fougasses —square wooden boxes filled with gunpowder— were buried in the ground about six inches from the surface. A small zinc tube enclosing a glass tube filled with a strong acid lay on the surface of the ground, lightly covered with earth or grass to hide it. When trodden upon the glass tube broke, and the acid escaping set fire to a piece of prepared match which communicated with the powder through a hollow wooden tube; the fougasse, or small mine, then blew up, killing or wounding those who happened to be near. We found a large number of fougasses between the Quarries and our advanced trench. Captain Cure, and those of his party who escaped untouched, returned to camp on the morning of the 8th, black with powder and very weary after their night's hard fighting. It was Cure's *baptême de feu*, a very hot one. Poor Thorley Stone's death was much felt by all in the regiment; he was such a bright, gallant young fellow, loved by all who knew him. The regiment was much disappointed to find that Colonel Campbell, the officer who commanded the attacking party, did not mention in his dispatch the prominent part taken by Captain Cure and the other officers and men of the 55th in the attack on the Quarries, and in holding the position during the night. A supplementary dispatch was sent in some time after rectifying the omission, and doing justice to the gallant behaviour of the officers and men of the 55th; but no rewards were given to the regiment.

The explanation of the mistake was that Colonel Campbell did not know that the 55th had been turned into part of the attacking party from being originally sent down as a working party; but the fact of their losing a fourth of their number ought to have shown the prominent part they took in the action.

On the 8th of June my brother Bob and I took a large party of the regiment into trenches. We occupied a part of the Russian works taken on the previous evening. Colonel Mauleverer, a fine soldier and a very good fellow, was field officer of the trenches. He was so thoughtful of and kind to me, as I felt very sad thinking of my poor young friend, Thorley Stone, lying dead up in camp. We spent rather a lively night, as the Russians resented our holding and making use of their works. They fired a great many shot and shell at us, and we had great difficulty in keeping under cover, as the works had not been reversed. The party of the 62nd, who were next us, had four of their senior officers knocked over by a round shot. Dickson and Foster were killed, and Sherman mortally and Ingall very severely wounded. Two of the 55th were killed by the same cannon-ball. Major James Daubeney (the late General James Daubeney, C.B.) had a very narrow escape—the shot grazed him. We had several men hit during the night. We were very glad to move out of our exposed position at daylight. Our batteries kept up a very heavy fire until 12 noon, when there was a truce for four hours to bury the dead. We saw a large number of dead Russians between the Quarries and the Redan; we found the ten men belonging to Elton's party, who had been reported missing, lying dead together. We all fraternised with the Russians who came to collect their dead. While we were talking to them a fougasse exploded, and both sides began to retire until the cause of alarm was explained. The Russian officers asked us "when we were going to take Sebastopol or leave the place." We could not give them the information they asked for, except that we did not intend to leave before we took Sebastopol. They seemed to be pleasant fellows, and we looked at them with interest, as they did at us. At four o'clock the truce ended, and both sides retired to their own works, and the batteries went at it again hammer and tongs. There were about seventy casualties in the right attack on the 8th.

Captain Mark Walker, who was promoted in May from the 30th into the 3rd Buffs, was dangerously wounded on the 9th of June, losing his right arm.

GENERAL SIR MARK WALKER, V.C., K.C.B.

My brother and I met him as he was being carried up to camp; we had known him for a long time when he was adjutant of the 30th; he was a gallant soldier and a capital officer; he distinguished himself on several occasions before he was wounded, and got the Victoria Cross. The 30th and 55th were always the best of friends, and we felt any losses they sustained almost as much as we did our own. The old friendship is still kept up whenever the two regiments meet—alas! under new names. I was often on trenches with Green, 30th Regiment. He was always called the "Count," a good fellow and a good officer. Nothing could put him out or make him hurry his movements. Even a shell pitching near him did not seem to affect his cool, deliberate manner. He was always the same, whether under fire or in his tent. Gubbins, another 30th officer, a tall, powerful man, distinguished himself greatly. On one occasion, when the Russians made a sortie, Gubbins went for them with a big stick, and laid about him with great effect until the Russians were driven off. He was an Irishman.

On the 12th of June ten men of the 55th were blown up by the explosion of a fougasse that had escaped the search on the 8th. Two were killed, the others were severely burnt. News came that

Anapa was taken and blown up. The mail came in with the Gazette. Cure got his majority, taking command of the 55th from Brevet-Lieut.-Colonel Cuddy, who was only senior captain. Cure commanded the regiment until the fall of Sebastopol. Richards got his company dated 1st of June. Cricket commenced about this time; we had some capital matches during the summer. The weather became very warm, and we found the trenches very trying, as we could not show our heads above the parapets to get a breath of air without being fired at. Most of us preferred the heat to the chance of being hit in the head. We had sun-shades made of canvas, but even under them we were baked; and swarms of flies annoyed us much. We used to dig holes and bury our bottles of beer, lemonade, and other drinks. After a time they became deliciously cool.

On the 15th of June Sir John Campbell and my brother Gustavus returned to camp from Kertch. They had a very pleasant time, and enjoyed the change much.

On the 16th Elton and I were on trenches in advance of the Quarries. The Russian trenches which we took on the 7th of June had been reversed, and we were saved a great deal of labour and much loss by the Russians having made these trenches. The enemy fired a good deal of grape at us during the night, and we were now near enough to their works to be presented with bouquets, which were composed of a number of small shells fired from a large mortar—very pretty to look at, but very unpleasant and difficult to avoid when they burst in all directions. Before we got so near the Russian works the French were the favoured recipients of bouquets.

Another unpleasant device of the enemy was to nearly fill a mortar with large grape-shot, and fire them into the air towards our trenches, where they would fall in an iron shower all about us. The first night they tried this we heard the report of a mortar fired in the Redan. We looked out as usual for a shell, but could see nothing. Presently we heard patter, patter all about, 2-pound grape-shot raining down upon us. It was impossible to get under cover from such a vertical shower, so we could only sit still and trust in Providence to shield us. Two of our men who were on sentry were killed the first time; their heads were cracked like egg-shells; some others were wounded. Always after this we were roused up at daybreak by a couple of showers of vertical grape. We did not like it, never getting used to it as we did to the other missiles; there was something uncanny about it. Poor Captain Johnnie Vaughan, 38th Regiment, in the left attack, was shot when visiting his sentries. He was deeply regretted by all who knew him.

On the 17th of June the fourth bombardment commenced. All the English and French batteries opened fire at an early hour, and the Russians replied, killing and wounding a considerable number of men in our works. Lieuts. Evans and Temple arrived with a draft for the 55th; both very nice young fellows. I bought poor Thorley Stone's favourite pony, a dark-grey barb called "Cossack"—a good match in size for my other barb, but a much more spirited animal. Some cases of cholera occurred in hospital. Still, the health of the troops was on the whole very good, and all were in good spirits, ready for anything. Rumours were flying about that the long looked-for and wished-for assault was decided upon, and all looked forward with the greatest confidence to the result. When Elton and I got back to camp, after thirty hours on trenches, we found all preparing for the attack which was to take place at daybreak. We got some dinner and forty winks, and then were ready to start again for the trenches.

## CHAPTER IX.

18TH OF JUNE—ATTACK ON SEBASTOPOL REPULSED—
HEAVY LOSSES — MAGAZINE SAVED BY CAPTAIN R.
HUME, SERGEANT TILTON, AND THREE MEN OF
THE LIGHT COMPANY, 55TH—GARNET WOLSELEY—
GENERAL LA MARMORA—DEATH OF LORD RAGLAN—
FUNERAL—BAIDAR VALLEY—GENERAL MARKHAM.

ON the morning of the 18th of June, soon after Elton and I came off trenches, the regiments of the 2nd Division paraded at 12.30 a.m. for the long looked-for assault on Sebastopol. The anniversary of Waterloo was, I believe, chosen so that the memory of that day might be to a certain extent wiped out by the capture of Sebastopol by the combined armies of England and France. It has been said, and I believe truly, that Lord Raglan and Marshal Pelissier had a difference of opinion as to the time the assault ought to take place and under what conditions. Lord Raglan considered that it was quite necessary that the Russian works should be bombarded for at least two hours before the assault took place, for, although the Russian defences had suffered much from the tremendous fire of the previous day, there had been time to repair damages and reinforce the hard-worked defenders with fresh troops. The result showed the wisdom of Lord Raglan's opinion. Unfortunately Marshal Pelissier thought otherwise, and he carried the day. Probably he thought that opening fire would put the Russians on their guard, whereas by attacking before daybreak they might be surprised before they had time to get reinforcements into their works. The 55th Regiment moved down into the first parallel to support the 41st, one of the regiments told off to storm the salient angle of the Great Redan. My brother and I with our companies, the Light and No. 6, were posted in the mortar battery on the extreme right of the first parallel, where we had a fine view of the French attack on the Malakoff. The Russians were evidently on the *qui vive*, as they at once opened fire on the advancing French, who, notwithstanding, moved gallantly forward for a certain distance, and then their lines of troops seemed to break up like waves dashing against rocks, and eventually all retired with a sad loss in officers and men. It was a grand

Maull & Fox, 187a, Piccadilly.]

**LIEUT.-COLONEL SIR GUSTAVUS HUME.**
*Lieutenant Royal Body Guard. Late 38th Regiment. Died 16th June, 1891.*

sight to watch the French advance under a regular *feu d'enfer*. The shells bursting amongst them could be seen quite plainly, owing to the want of light. Some, but not many, French reached the Malakoff, where they were either shot down or taken prisoners. Soon after the French began their attack the British troops got orders to attack the Great Redan, but like the French at the Malakoff, they were driven back by the heavy fire from the Russian batteries, having a long way to go before reaching the abattis in front of the salient angle of the Redan. The Light Division suffered very severely. Colonel Yea, 7th Fusiliers, a very gallant and distinguished officer, was killed early in the attack. The 34th suffered terribly, losing four officers and fifty men killed, and six officers and 260 men wounded. The 4th Division suffered great loss. Sir John Campbell, who commanded the 4th Division, sent his two aides-de-camp, Captain Gustavus Hume and Captain Snodgrass, away to deliver some messages. As soon as they were gone Sir John moved out of the trench at the head of some of his division, leading them towards the Redan; he had not gone far when he was killed, struck by a grape-shot. My brother, finding on his return from delivering the message that Sir John had gone to the front,

rushed after him, but could not find him. He
searched for some time and had many narrow
escapes. At last he returned to the trenches with
some of the remains of the stormers. The 2nd
Division did not leave the trenches, as our general,
when he saw the hopelessness of the attack, wisely
saved his division from adding to the already very
heavy list of killed and wounded. The 55th were
waiting for the order to advance, but it never
came. But even under cover we were not safe,
as the Russians kept up a heavy fire on our
trenches. A shell pitched on a heap of carcasses
close to the door of the magazine of the mortar
battery, where my brother and I were with our
companies. The shell burst, setting the carcasses
alight. All thought that the magazine was on
fire, and most of us at first tried to get away
from its vicinity. My brother, with Sergeant
Tilton and three men of the Light Company,
whose names I regret to say I have forgotten,
remained, and seizing some shovels, heaped earth
on the burning mass, until all danger to the
magazine was over, and thereby, in all probability,
saving great loss of life, which must have taken
place had the magazine blown up. We all marched
back to camp very sad as we thought of the
great loss of officers and men that had taken

place to no purpose. The attack on the left under General Eyre was successful up to a certain point, and would have been of the greatest use had the general attack succeeded. His force suffered great loss in officers and men, especially in the 38th, 44th, and 18th Regiments. We lost four great friends in the 44th—Captains Agar, Caulfield, Fenwick, and Mansfield; they were all mortally wounded in the cemetery. Colonel the Hon. Augustus Spencer commanding the 44th was wounded, and several others.

The cemetery was taken and held. Captain Fisher, Royal Engineers, an old Gibraltar friend, led some of the stormers as far as the abattis in front of the Redan and greatly distinguished himself. He escaped without a wound, and brought back a number of the survivors. Another Gibraltar friend, Lieut. Graves, Royal Engineers, was killed close to the Redan. The British loss on the 18th of June was about 1,500, the French about 3,400, and the Russian was said to be 5,400. The Naval Brigade greatly distinguished themselves. Our advance trench was too far from the Redan to give any body of men a chance of reaching the work in any kind of formation under the very heavy fire of round shot, shell, and grape. The only wonder was that any men who reached the abattis escaped unhurt.

On the night of the 18th some men of the 1st Division occupied the parallels in rear of the advance, and being new to the trenches, they forgot that men of the 2nd and Light Divisions were in their front; so when, during the night, the Russians opened fire, the 1st Division fired in return, quite regardless of our men in their front. Fortunately they fired high, so did us no harm. Probably they hit some of the enemy in Sebastopol.

On the 19th there was a truce for two hours for collecting and burying the dead. Some of us went to poor Agar's and Caulfield's funerals, and afterwards to that of Sir John Campbell. A very large number of officers attended. Sir John was a fine soldier and a great favourite with officers and men. My brother Gustavus lost a good and dear friend when he was killed. I often met Captain Garnet Wolseley, 90th Regiment (now Viscount Wolseley, G.C.B., &c., &c.), in the trenches during the siege. We were both in the right attack, and were good friends in those days. He was an acting engineer, and was a very energetic, plucky officer. One little thought then that he would rise to the high rank and honours that he has since attained to. He was wise in his generation, and elected to stick to staff employ instead of remaining a regimental officer, which might not lead to more than the command of a regiment. I have not seen very much of him since the old Crimean days, and expect he can hardly remember many of those he knew at that time. He distinguished himself on several occasions, and was severely wounded before the end of the siege.

On the 23rd of June my brother Bob bought a horse that belonged to Sir John Campbell, a fine, strong animal. He rode him with Cure and me to Komara, where we saw some fine views from a Sardinian outpost. The Tchatir Dagh, the highest mountain in the Crimea, in shape not unlike Gibraltar, was one of the chief features in the distance. We saw some of the Sardinian army, well-dressed, soldier-like men. I had seen them land a short time before, a very compact little army of over 10,000 men, under the command of General La Marmora. They were well provided with transport, and had everything very complete. I met General La Marmora many years after, in 1874, at Wildbad. He was greatly pleased when I spoke to him about the army he commanded in the Crimea. Talking to him about short service and officers and men, knowing each other well, he said, "I would rather, in battle, command 100,000 men I did know than 400,000 I did not know." He had just come from the manœuvres on Salisbury Plain, and was loud in his praises of our artillery. He gave me a pressing invitation to visit him at Florence, but he died soon after leaving Wildbad, before I went to Italy.

Lord Raglan felt the disaster of the 18th of June keenly. He was attacked with diarrhœa, which turned to cholera. He died on the 28th of June, deeply regretted by the whole allied army. He was a fine, brave, chivalrous English gentleman, courteous to all. His great friend, General Estcourt, died a few days before his chief. Lord Raglan's funeral was on the 3rd of July. It was a very fine and impressive sight, attended by all the principal officers of the allied armies; amongst others Pelissier, Omar Pacha, and La Marmora were conspicuous. I was on duty with fifty men of the 55th, so had a good view of the sad procession as it passed close to me. Lieut.-General Sir James Simpson succeeded to the command of the British army before Sebastopol on Lord Raglan's death.

All through July and until the end of the siege our nights in the trenches were pretty lively as a rule. The Russians kept us awake with shot, shell, grape, and bouquets at intervals They had a playful way of sending up two mortar shells followed by two others immediately after, so that there were four in the air at the same time. It was very difficult to dodge them, as they all seemed to come straight for any place we might be, and to follow us wherever we ran for safety. I used generally to lie down and trust that the shells would not fall upon me. Sometimes they would pitch within a few yards and then burst. It was marvellous how few men were hit in proportion to the number and variety of missiles that were fired at us. We got pretty well accustomed to them, as it is said "eels do to skinning;" but none of us thoroughly enjoyed the excitement. We lost several of our Grenadier company, shot through the head, as the parapets were very low in some places, and a tall man had no chance of being hidden unless he stooped. Many men would not take the trouble to stoop, or forgot to do so, and came to grief in consequence.

On the 14th of July we placed a stone cross on poor Thorley Stone's grave. There were many fresh graves since he was buried on the 9th of June. One day Cuddy, Cure, Elton, and I took a long ride, about fifteen miles, through the Baidar Pass into the Baidar Valley. The day was perfect, and we had a lovely ride. The scenery was beautiful, and the change from a warlike to a perfectly peaceful scene was delightful. We all felt as if we should like to ride on instead of returning to the monotonous existence in camp and constant sound of the siege guns. We rested near a very prettily situated villa belonging to some Russian nobleman, which was surrounded by woods. The villa was not much when we got close to it; it looked better from a distance. The views from it were lovely—at least we thought them so after looking so long at Sebastopol. We got back to camp about seven o'clock refreshed in mind and body.

My brother Gustavus, who had not been at all well, got short leave to go to Constantinople. My brother Walter, 38th Regiment, arrived in camp at the beginning of July, riding a very small pony which he bought in Asia Minor, near Troy. He called it "Trojan." It was the smallest pony in camp, but was wonderfully strong and useful. We were now four brothers at the siege, two in the right and two in the left attacks, two in the 38th and two in the 55th Regiments. Walter had a narrow escape the first time he went on trenches: a large piece of shell struck the hilt of his sword, denting it considerably. I paid Walker, 3rd Buffs, a visit, and found him sitting up minus his right arm. He was very cheery, getting on capitally. One of our men was flogged for shirking trenches: he was a fine-looking man, but was constantly absent from camp when his turn came for trench guard. He had been

CAPTAIN WALTER HUME.
*Late 38th and 75th Regiments.*

flogged several times, always for the same offence. He volunteered from the 55th to his old regiment during the Mutiny, and did splendid service in India, quite wiping out his bad record in the Crimea.

On the 11th of July Elton and I went on trenches. I see that I have described the march down as a "perilous one" in my diary. The Russians fired on our party the whole way down. We had two men killed and several wounded, and we had many narrow escapes before we reached our post in the advance. I always felt thankful when my tour of duty in trenches was over, as one never felt safe even when under cover. When we returned to camp on the morning of the 12th I found Colonel Warren in my tent: he had just returned from England, quite recovered from his wound. He was made Brigadier-General, and took Lieut. Morgan, 55th, as his A.D.C. Major-General Markham, 32nd Regiment, arrived from India and took command of the 2nd Division, General Pennefather having left some time before. Major-General Markham was a very good, smart officer but was not in good health when he arrived in the Crimea. He made a very long, rapid journey from up country in India. He was severely hurt by a kick from a camel while on his journey, never quite recovering from the effects. He died at

Malta very soon after the fall of Sebastopol. He was a great shikari and a very soldier-like-looking man. Lieut. Augustus King, Royal Artillery (now Major-General King) was General Markham's A.D.C. His brother, Captain King, 32nd Regiment, died of cholera at Balaclava soon after he landed in the Crimea.

Our time now was pretty well occupied with trenches, working parties, parades for drill, cricket, and riding about the country. The weather was perfect, and life would have been very enjoyable only for the uncertainty of what a day might bring forth. That part of the army that had no trench work had a nice easy time every night in bed, and nothing but the ordinary peace routine to get through—very different from those who were continually going down to trenches, running great risks, and in the end getting no more in the shape of reward than those who were as safe as if they were stationed in England, except when there was a big fight, when they took part in it. I have always thought that there should have been some special recognition for constant work in trenches for those who bore the burden and heat of the siege. I think if Lord Raglan had lived he would have done his best to get the home authorities to consider the subject.

## CHAPTER X.

COOKING—LIVELY NIGHT IN TRENCHES—HEAVY RAIN—GEESE—PICNIC TO BAIDAR VALLEY—ELTON'S BRAVERY — DEATH OF LIEUT. EVANS — ELTON WOUNDED—BATTLE OF TCHERNAYA—CRICKET—SORTIE—SALVOES.

MY brother Gustavus sent our mess a grand hamper of vegetables from Constantinople—a most acceptable present. Lieut.-Colonel Cuddy used to make first-rate vegetable devils, and his anchovy toast was quite the best I ever tasted. His talents as a cook added much to the success of our little dinners. Colonel Daubeney was also a first-rate cook, and when we were in Bulgaria the Grenadier mess benefited much by having two such cooks belonging to it. I am quite of opinion that every officer ought to be taught in his youth how to cook a few things really well, for his own as well as other people's benefit.

On the 23rd of July brother Gustavus returned from leave. He was appointed Deputy Adjutant-General, 3rd Division. Colonel Thackwell (now General Thackwell, C.B.) was his chief. He was a real good fellow and a capital officer. He had been on the staff of the 2nd Division with General Pennefather and distinguished himself at Alma and Inkerman. We were all very sorry when he left the 2nd Division. Brothers Gus and Walter frequently dined with us. We were a very cheery lot together, being always a most united band of brothers.

On the 24th five officers and two hundred men of the 55th went on trenches, and we had a real lively time, as the Russians opened a very heavy fire on us from all the batteries that were opposite the right attack. Why they treated us to such a cannonade on this occasion no one could make out, unless they expected an assault. A round shot struck the parapet where I was sitting, knocking the gabions over and burying a lot of us under the *débris*. I was trampled upon and bruised, and five men were killed and wounded. I was not much damaged.

On the 29th of July there was some very heavy rain. Elton and I were on trenches, and found them nearly knee deep in mud and water. The enemy would not leave us alone; they fired heavily on us, killing and wounding ten of our party. We seldom went down to trenches without having some casualties. There was some very heavy rain on the 31st of July. The weather cleared up in the afternoon, and we were able to have a cricket match. My brother made 44 not out, I made 8. Our side won by five wickets.

On the 1st of August General Markham began his inspection of the 55th and finished on the 7th. He was pleased on the whole, especially with the appearance of the men. He could not expect us to turn out exactly as if we were in barracks at home. There was a terrific storm of rain on the 7th of August; it came down in torrents. Small rushing rivers ran down the ravines. Some of the men were carried off their legs on their way to trenches; two were very nearly drowned. Our camp was deep in mud after the storm, and the trenches were in a dreadful state. I rode with Capel Cure to Balaclava to buy some stores for the mess. In addition to other things we bought twelve geese, which we tied up somehow to our saddles. On our way back to camp we passed close to a pond. Some of our geese got loose, and we had great difficulty in catching them. Poor things, they did enjoy their bath.

We used to tether our geese outside our tents and feed them on biscuit until they became fat. They were excellent eating.

In the beginning of August about thirty officers of the 2nd Division started for a picnic to the Baidar Valley. We had a delightful and most amusing ride; every one was in tremendous spirits, and we were all like a lot of emancipated schoolboys. Captain Cooch, 62nd Regiment (now Lieut.-Colonel one of the Royal Body Guard), says that I broke his little finger when we were skylarking. Whenever I meet him he holds up his hand—and certainly his finger is rather crooked. We lunched close to the Russian Count's villa, under the shade of some trees, where we had a fine view of the valley, which looked beautiful. The day was warm and bright, and all thoroughly enjoyed the outing. My brother Bob and others sang, and we had no end of choruses. The ride home was very enjoyable for every one except Cure, whose horse broke loose, ran away, and was never recovered—a serious matter when fifteen miles from home. I forget how Cure got home, but imagine he got an occasional lift on some one else's horse. My diary records that next morning a number of brandies and sodas were consumed, so I fancy

LIEUT.-COLONEL F. C. ELTON, V.C.
*Late 55th and 21st Regiments.*

our ride home must have been a dry and dusty one.

On the night of the 4th of August Elton, Johnson, Evans, and I went on a working party. Elton and Evans with half the party were in the advance, Johnson and I were some way in rear. We had a very hot night of it, the Russians firing incessantly. Elton's party had to connect one part of the advanced trench with another—a very necessary piece of work which the engineers were most anxious should be completed before daylight. The Russians did all they could to prevent the work being done; they fired heavily on Elton's party, obliging them to take shelter. Elton then went out alone with a pickaxe, setting to work as an example to his men. They soon joined him, and the work was completed under a heavy fire of grape and other shot. Poor Evans was mortally wounded, and eighteen men were wounded, some very severely. Elton got the Victoria Cross for his bravery on this and another occasion. His men said that "very few in the British army would have done what Captain Elton did." I had very few casualties amongst my party: we were not exposed in the same way as Elton's men were. Lieut. Evans died on the morning of the 6th, after dreadful suffering; he was hit in the throat by a grape-shot. Everything possible was done to save his life, but in vain. He was a very nice young fellow, liked by all who knew him. He was buried on Cathcart's hill at the same time as Colonel Cobbe, 4th Regiment. Captain Layard, 38th Regiment, who was on the staff of the 2nd Division, died on board ship at Balaclava. He was an excellent officer and a very good fellow. He was a brother of Nineveh Layard. We were all very sorry for him.

On the 11th of August Elton was on trenches. He was lying down in a safe place. A shell burst near him: a piece of it struck him in the breast, inflicting a very painful but not a dangerous wound. He had a small prayer-book in the breast of his coatee: fortunately the piece of shell struck it, cutting through the binding and most of the leaves. The book most likely saved Elton's life. He was sent to the monastery of St. George, where he remained until he was fit for duty. Surgeon Blake (55th) was there for some time very unwell.

Cure, Temple, and I were on trenches on the 13th of August. The firing was as usual very heavy: we had one man killed and several wounded. The 2nd Division played a cricket match against the cavalry, beating them by forty-seven runs. It was a capital game; I made ten runs.

On the 16th of August, the anniversary of my birthday, we were kept in readiness all day to turn out at a moment's notice. The French and Sardinians were attacked by the Russians, under General Read, at Tchorgoum, on the Tchernaya. After a severe fight the Russians were defeated with great loss, and driven back to the Mackenzie heights. General Read was killed; the Russian loss was great. Hamley puts it down—3 generals, 66 other officers, and 2,300 men killed, 160 officers and 4,000 men wounded; in addition to these, 31 officers and 1,700 men had disappeared—where to is not shown. The French lost only 1,500 killed and wounded; the Sardinians 200. I rode over the field of battle a few days after the action, and saw all the different positions.

I went on trenches on the 17th of August. We expended a tremendous amount of ammunition during the night, as our men had orders to keep up a constant fire on the embrasures of the Redan, to prevent the enemy repairing damages. I believe we annoyed them very considerably, and in revenge they treated us now and then to a lively cannonade, which amused them and did us very little harm.

As there seemed to be every probability that we should spend the next winter before Sebastopol, I began to get my tent dug out. It was a hard piece of work owing to the rocky ground, but when finished it made a very comfortable abode, with a place for a stove and cupboards all round, let into the walls. I was rather proud of my tent when it was finished.

The Russians used to fire long shots from guns sunk in the ground, with their muzzles much elevated. Several round shot came into our camp: one fell on a table at which two officers were seated: the table was smashed to pieces. The officers escaped unhurt, but were rather alarmed at the unwarrantable intrusion. Another shot fell on the general's stable, killing a charger belonging to his A.D.C., Lieut. Augustus King.

On the 24th of August the 2nd Division played a return match against the cavalry, beating them, after a most exciting match, by two wickets. The cavalry were most hospitable, keeping us well supplied with cool drinks, which were most acceptable, as the day was most uncommonly warm.

On the night of the 1st of September the Russians made a sortie on the right attack. As usual they were repulsed, but not before they had done a good deal of damage. Our side had

LIEUT.-COLONEL H. BURKE.
*Late 55th Regiment.*

several casualties: Captain Frazer, 95th, was killed; Lieut. Forbes, Adjutant, 30th Regiment, was mortally wounded; Captain Ross, 3rd Buffs, was taken prisoner; another officer of the Buffs wounded, and several men were killed and wounded.

Lieut. Burke and I went on trenches on the night of the 2nd of September. We were on the advance. My men and I had rather an unpleasant time, having to go out in front as a covering party to a working party. I had seventy men with me. The Russians crept up a ravine on our right, and fired on my party. The men, in the trenches behind us, forgetting, no doubt, that we were in their immediate front, fired in return, so we had the benefit of the fire from friends and foes. Lieut. Elphinstone, Royal Engineers (the late Sir Howard Elphinstone, V.C., K.C.B.), who was in front with some sappers laying some gabions, joined my party, and we retired together, leaving the gabions. I had a corporal killed and six men wounded—whether by friends or foes I could not say. It was a very unpleasant experience, quite a case of "save me from my friends." Many more would have been hit if Burke and I had not made them lie down until the firing ceased. About this time the French began to try a new phase in bombarding. Every day, at about twelve o'clock, at a given signal, they would fire a salvo of about 250 guns at the same time. It had a grand effect to lookers-on, but to the Russians it was a veritable *feu d'enfer*, as they afterwards described it, and the damage done by such a weight of metal being thrown into the enemy's works was great. Those shot that missed the works went into the town. I used to watch for the salvoes when everything was quite still during the great heat in the middle of the day. Suddenly I would see a long line of smoke, and then there would be a roar that shook the ground. A thick cloud of dust along the Russian works showed where the iron shower fell, and then all would be still until the next salvo. Rumours began to fly about that the assault would soon take place.

Our old friends, the 13th, Prince Albert's Light Infantry, under the command of Lord Mark Kerr, came up to the front from Balaclava on the 4th of September. I saw them disembark at Balaclava, Lord Mark riding about on one of the hottest days with his shako in his hand. He cared as little for the sun as he did for the enemy. The 13th had been quartered with us at Gibraltar for three years.

On the 5th of September my brother Bob and I took our last ride together in the Crimea. We rode to Balaclava up to the camp of the Marines, round by Komara and the Traktir Bridge, the scene of the battle of the 16th of August. Many traces of the fight could still be seen. In the evening a large vessel was burnt in Sebastopol harbour.

On the 7th of September Bissett, who was wounded at the Alma, rejoined the 55th, with a draft of fifty men. The French batteries fired heavily on the 6th and 7th, firing salvoes in addition to keeping up a general cannonade. Two small mines were exploded by the French close up to the Malakoff. They had worked up to within a very short distance of that work, losing a great number of men every twenty-four hours. The enemy resented the French getting to such close quarters, as they must have felt that the end was drawing nigh. We were no nearer the Redan than we were on the 18th of June. The nature of the ground prevented our working any closer, and our advance parallel was quite 250 yards from the salient angle of the Redan. We heard that the assault was to take place at noon on the 8th of September, and that the 2nd and Light Divisions were to have the honour of furnishing the stormers and supports for the attack on the Great Redan, the only point that was to be attacked by the British army. Of course we appreciated the compliment very much; it was kindly meant; but at the same time we could not help thinking that those divisions which had had comparatively little fighting, and which were largely composed of fine old veterans who had landed in the Crimea on the 14th of September, 1854, ought to have been given a chance of distinguishing themselves. We had a dinner party at our mess on the eve of the assault. Brothers Gustavus and Walter dined with us, and the four brothers parted about ten o'clock, not knowing what the morrow would bring forth.

## CHAPTER XI.

8TH OF SEPTEMBER—ATTACK ON SEBASTOPOL—FRENCH TAKE MALAKOFF—CAPTAIN R. HUME BLOWN UP—BRITISH ATTACK ON GREAT REDAN — PRIVATES WHELAN AND DUNN, 55TH REGIMENT—BRIGADIER-GENERAL WINDHAM—HEAVY LOSSES—RETREAT—I AM WOUNDED—DEATH OF LIEUT.-COLONEL CUDDY—END OF SIEGE.

THE 8th of September, 1855, was a bright but stormy day, with clouds of dust flying about —a great advantage, as it turned out, for it prevented the Russians seeing the movements of the troops while marching to their various posts in the trenches. All got there unobserved by the enemy. The 55th Regiment, under Major Alfred Capel Cure (Brevet-Lieut.-Colonel W. H. L. D. Cuddy being second in command), was told off as a part of the 2nd Division supports to the stormers. We moved off soon after breakfast, arriving at our appointed place in the advanced parallel about 10.30 a.m.

My company, No. 6, was formed in rear of the Light Company commanded by my brother, Captain R. Hume. We were told off to lead the regiment when the supports got the order to advance. The salient angle of the Great Redan was the point we were ordered to make for. All thought that as far as the arrangements for the British attack went, they were in many ways similar to those of the 18th of June, as on the 8th of September we were no nearer the Redan than on the former occasion, and the same 250 yards had to be passed over without a particle of cover before the salient angle could be reached. But " ours not to reason why," so we waited impatiently for the order to advance. There was one great difference I ought to mention, viz., that our batteries had been firing heavily on the Russian works from an early hour, whereas on the 18th of June the attack was made without the preliminary bombardment. While waiting, some of us read our prayer-books. After reading I put mine in the breast of my coatee: I may have thought that it might stop a bullet. Just before we got the order to advance a shell from the enemy fell amongst us, burying itself in the trench close to my brother. Private O'Brien, of the Light Company, seeing the shell pitch, pulled my brother down to try and save him; the shell exploded under my brother and blew him some paces down the trench, wounding him severely, but not dangerously. I had not time to speak to him before I got the order to take our two companies out to support the stormers, who had reached the Redan and were hotly engaged. The remaining companies of the 55th were to follow as soon as they could be brought up. There was only room enough in the trench to form up two companies at a time. I sprang over the parapet followed by the Light Company and No. 6, and we made our way across the space between our trenches and the Redan as quickly as we could under a very heavy fire of round shot, shell, and grape. Several men were knocked over. A grape-shot struck me on the breast, glanced off my prayer-book, cutting through my sword-belt, and denting the Light Company whistle which was on my belt, but beyond the shock doing me no harm. Fortunately I was waving my sword at the time or I must have been struck in the right arm. Part of my water-bottle was shot away soon after; it was hanging by my side. On arriving at the Redan I found the salient angle crowded with men of various regiments, the stormers who had been driven back. Some had penetrated into the Redan, but the fire from the flanks of the work was too much for them, broken up as they were by having to cross the 250 yards under a very heavy fire. Some had stopped short under cover instead of rushing the work, and they impeded those who came after them. I found it quite impossible to get my men through the crowd on the salient in any kind of formation, so the only thing to be done was to get through as best we could; but it was fatal to our chance of doing much to be stopped in our advance, and whatever formation we had was quite destroyed; it was too late, under the heavy fire we were exposed to, to try another part of the work. I, with some of my men, went down one of the scaling ladders and up another until we got near the crest of the parapet. Two of my men, real plucky fellows, got through the crowd on to the crest and helped me up. They were both Irishmen, Privates Jeremiah Whelan and James Dunn. When I got up I had a good view of the interior of the Redan, and saw a number of our men lying dead where they had been killed by the fire from the flanks of the work and some guns in rear. There were no Russians to be seen in my immediate front, but I could see numbers behind the traverses on either flank, and they kept up a hot fire upon us. Whelan said to me, "Ah, sir, let us charge them!" I turned to the men of various regiments behind me who were crowding the salient angle, and said, "If these men will go with us we will; three of us are not enough to do any good." They did not respond. My men kept firing into the Russians quite coolly, and it was a marvel how they escaped being killed. I noticed a fine tall Russian officer about twenty-five yards from us on our right front. He was quite in the open. He had loaded muskets handed up to him, which he fired at us as quickly as he could. Whelan said, "Sir, there's a fine shot for your revolver." I wanted to keep my shot for closer quarters, so told Whelan he had better shoot him; and I believe he did, as the brave Russian disappeared, apparently shot. It was a pity, but as he was killing our men it was a relief to get rid of him. I hope he was only wounded. A Russian threw either a hand grenade or a stone, which hit me on the back of my head, knocking me down under a scaling ladder. A man of the 41st Regiment, shot through the head, fell over me, and I had some difficulty in getting out of a very unpleasant place, as I was a bit bothered by the blow on my head. Private Dunn came to me with a bullet-hole right through his shoulder. He said to me when he was hit, "Ah, sir, I'm done at last!" I don't think he meant to make a joke on his name. He did not die, but lost his arm out of the socket. Private Whelan escaped unhurt. Both were given the French war medal for valour.

I managed to get back across the ditch, and lay down for a time with some men of the 55th, who were firing at any Russians who showed themselves. If reinforcements had been sent out in proper numbers when we were holding the salient angle I firmly believe that the Redan would have been taken and held, and England and the British army would have been saved the mortification of hearing that the French had succeeded and we had failed. If the Highland Brigade, whose ranks were filled with splendid old soldiers, had been sent at the Redan when it was seen that the salient angle was held, but that there was no chance of the work being carried, they would, I feel certain, have swept all before them, and those of the first attacking party that were left would have joined the Highlanders, and the Russians would have been driven out. Major Cure wished to take the 55th out in a body, not to send it out in driblets, but was ordered by one of the generals to send out the two companies, the Light and No. 6, at once. He then waited for the other six companies. They never came, having most probably been taken out by their officers before arriving at the place where Major Cure was waiting. At last he took out all the men he could collect, about enough to make one company, and joined the rest at the Redan, where he found Lieut.-Colonel Cuddy and a mixed crowd of men from various regiments. After consulting with Colonel Cuddy, Major Cure went back to our trenches to try and bring out the remainder of the regiment, but could not find them, as they were most of them already at the Redan. He then returned, crossing a second time under the heavy fire of the enemy, and was severely wounded by a musket-ball which broke his arm. After remaining some time with his men his wound grew painful, and he returned to our lines, and was sent home by Surgeon Gordon. Poor Lieut.-Colonel Cuddy was shot dead in the ditch of the Redan soon after taking over the command of the 55th from Major Cure, and many of our non-commissioned officers and privates were killed and wounded. Shortly after I recrossed the ditch a portion of the earth of the salient angle collapsed with the men that were on it, and then all who were able began to retire, but not before two-thirds of the attacking force were killed and wounded, upwards of 2,000 out of 3,000 —a large proportion. Lieuts. Harkness, Johnson, and Roxby, 55th, were close to me on the parapet of the Redan, with several men of their companies, remaining until the column retired. The Russians, when they saw us retreating, jumped up on the parapets, cheering loudly. They threw everything they could lay hands on after us, and shot down a great number before we could reach our trenches. A musket-ball smashed my left arm. I always said, " If I am to be hit I should like it to be in the left arm, and on the last day of the siege," and so it fortunately turned out. Lieut. Johnson, 55th, was severely wounded in the ankle. A Russian threw his musket and bayonet at him. Captain Richards was also wounded. Bugler Doyle, 55th, distinguished himself much, and was given the Cross of the Legion of Honour.

I managed after I was wounded to get back to our trenches. Captain Atcherley, 30th Regiment, kindly stopped to help me. On getting over the parapet into our lines I met Colonel Windham, who was about to return with a regiment to reinforce the column at the Redan. I told him that it was of no use his going on, as all who could had retired. He did not go. He was in command of the attacking force, and after being at the Redan for some time, and having sent for reinforcements, which did not arrive, he, seeing that his force could not take and hold the work, went back himself to try and get more men. Whether he did right or wrong to leave his command I cannot say. No one ever doubted his courage. It may have been an error of judgment, but no doubt he meant it for the best, knowing that if he could bring up sufficient fresh troops the work might be held. One regiment would not have been enough. If, as I said before, the general commanding had sent the Highland Brigade forward when he saw that the attack had partially failed, the Redan would have been ours. When the French took the Malakoff I could see the Russians streaming from that work towards the Redan, and as Sir Edward Hamley says: "It was unfortunate that the French had spiked the guns in the Malakoff instead of turning them on the enemy moving into the Redan, as they ought to have done." There is no doubt that the men of the 2nd and Light Divisions, who had borne the burden and heat of the trench work from the commencement to the end of the siege, ought to have been the reserve instead of being the attacking force. There were numbers of young soldiers in the two divisions who had been taught to keep under cover as much as possible when in trenches, who on reaching the Redan sought for cover instead of rushing the work. The 1st

Division, fine old soldiers who had not done as much trench work, would most likely have taken the Redan and held it, but the great distance between our works and the Russian work was one of the principal causes of our failure. It was impossible to keep any steady formation under the very heavy fire we were exposed to while crossing the 250 yards, and there not being sufficient space in our trenches to allow of more than two companies to be formed up at a time, obliged us to move out in driblets instead of in a strong column such as is usual in an attack on a strong position. The British loss of 2,200 killed and wounded, out of about 3,000, shows the heavy fire we were exposed to. I do not think that Colonel Windham's leaving his command had anything to do with the retiring of the remnant of the attacking force, who, seeing that it was hopeless to attempt to hold the Redan without reinforcements, and finding that they were suffering heavily, apparently to no purpose, retreated, and thereby prevented greater loss.

Ordering us all to assault the salient angle instead of making attacks on several points of the Redan, and thereby distracting the attention of the enemy, and preventing them concentrating their fire on one point, would seem to be a mistake, but no doubt the reasons were good, and if the attack in the first instance had succeeded, and the supports had found the salient angle clear, it was the part least exposed to the enemy's fire. Brigadier-General Warren and his aide-de-camp, Lieutenant Morgan, 55th Regiment, were both wounded, the latter very severely. His arm was broken in two places by a blow from a rifle which was knocked out of a man's hand by a round shot. The 55th had 1 officer killed and 7 wounded, 2 corporals and 24 men killed, 8 sergeants, 14 corporals, and 92 privates wounded, making a total of 8 officers and 140 non-commissioned officers and privates killed and wounded. The only attack that succeeded on the 8th of September was that of the French on the Malakoff. They were so close to that work that they took it with very little loss. They took the enemy completely by surprise, whereas when the English attacked the Redan the Russians were quite prepared. The Malakoff being a complete work, closed at the gorge, enabled the French to hold it against any odds. They lost heavily in the several attempts the Russians made to retake the work. The French attacks on the left were all repulsed by the Russians with great loss. The French losses on the 8th were about 7,500 officers and men, the

English about 2,270, and the Russians nearly 13,000. Out of the 2nd Division cricket eleven who played in a match against the 4th Division on the 1st of September seven were killed and wounded. The four bowlers were killed.

As soon as I had my wound dressed I walked about two miles through the trenches until I found an ambulance car, which took me and other wounded to camp, where I found Major Cure and my brother in bed, as comfortable as they could be under the circumstances. They had one of the few huts that had been erected. After I saw them and had a talk I went to my tent, where some of the surgeons of the 2nd Division held a consultation as to whether my arm was to be amputated. They all agreed that it ought to be cut off with the exception of Cowan, our assistant-surgeon, a clever young Scotchman, who said, "I know Captain Hume's constitution and habits, and think I can save his arm ; at all events, leave it on until to-morrow." The others agreed, and I owe the saving of my arm to the old regimental system of having surgeons belonging to regiments who know the habits and constitutions of officers and men from constant observation. I mentioned this before.

We all felt the death of Brevet-Lieut.-Colonel Cuddy very much. He was a gallant soldier, a true friend, and a good man in every way. It was very sad that he should be killed after going through the campaign from beginning to end. He commanded the 55th from Inkerman until the 8th of June, when Major Cure took over the command. The 55th Regiment owed much to Lieut.-Colonel Cuddy, and also to Surgeon Ethelbert Blake, who worked with him, for the admirable way the regiment was looked after and brought through the trying winter of 1854-1855. It was a pleasure to serve under such a commanding officer—thoughtful and kind, and at the same time strict in all matters of duty. I lost several great friends on the 8th: Patullo and Stevenson, 30th Regiment; Tyler and Blakiston, 62nd, the four best bowlers in the 2nd Division; Colonel Eman, 41st, a fine officer and a charming fellow, and others. Many had very narrow escapes. Hugh Rowlands, 41st, was wounded and had a bullet through his forage cap just above the grenade; Moorsom, 30th, was severely wounded. I found my tent which I had dug out and made comfortable for the winter, a capital abode, and I lay in it on the night of the 8th and morning of the 9th of September listening to the explosions which took place at intervals in Sebastopol. I was delighted to hear that the Russians had evacuated the south side. The

Redan fell into our hands without any further loss, and the great siege of Sebastopol was at an end.

I was nearly a month in bed before I was able to sit up. At first I suffered a good deal from my arm, but I soon got accustomed to it. Numbers of friends visited me every day, and all were most kind. General Barnard sent me grapes, &c. My brothers Gustavus and Walter came constantly to see me. Walter brought me fine fat quail which he shot in the neighbourhood of the camp. Major Cure and my brother Robert were sufficiently recovered to leave the Crimea on the 5th of October. I was very sorry not to be able to accompany them, but the doctors would not allow me. Among my visitors were my cousins, Henry Brooke, 48th Regiment, a good and gallant officer, who was killed as brigadier-general when commanding a sortie from Kandahar, the Hon. Robert Handcock, 48th Regiment, and his brother, the Hon. Henry Handcock, 44th Regiment, who was killed by a tiger in India. Their uncle, Colonel the Hon. Henry Handcock, was killed on the 8th of September at the Redan.

## CHAPTER XII.

ARM-SLING WORKED BY THE QUEEN—I AM CONVALESCENT—LEAVE FOR ENGLAND—55TH UNTIL END OF CAMPAIGN—LOSSES DURING THE CAMPAIGN—REWARDS—LOSS OF NUMBERS AND CHANGE OF NAME—REMARKS ABOUT 55TH—CONCLUSION.

THERE was a great ceremony at headquarters for the investiture of the Bath. General Simpson, the commander-in-chief, received six arm-slings, worked by Her Majesty the Queen, which she sent out to the Crimea to be given to wounded officers. Sir James Simpson asked Brigadier-General Charles Windham, who was with the 2nd Division, if there was any officer in the division he would like to give one of the arm-slings to. General Windham said, "Yes, I should like to take one to Captain Jack Hume." Some one said, "You mean Captain Robert Hume." He replied, "No, it would not be of much use to him, as he was hit in the leg. I mean his brother, whose arm was broken." General Windham brought the sling straight from headquarters to my tent and gave it to me. I felt very proud at getting such a valuable gift. I wore the sling at the first levee I attended after my return to England. When going down on my knee to kiss the Queen's hand the hilt of my sword caught in the sling and prevented my getting down. Her Majesty most graciously stepped forward and gave me her hand, saying some kind words to me as she helped me up. In 1877, when I was quartered at Portsmouth in command of the 55th Regiment, I asked Sir Hastings Doyle, commanding the division, if he thought he could obtain Her Majesty's signature to the arm-sling. He very kindly sent it to Sir Henry Ponsonby to Balmoral, he took it to the Queen, who was graciously pleased to accede to the request, writing the following on a piece of parchment paper and gumming it on to the sling, "Worked by Victoria Reg., 1855."

I was able to sit up on the 4th of October, and was soon able to get out. One of the first men I met walking about was Private James Dunn, minus his arm, which had been amputated. I managed to ride "Bazouk" down into Sebastopol, where I lunched with the four town majors at the great

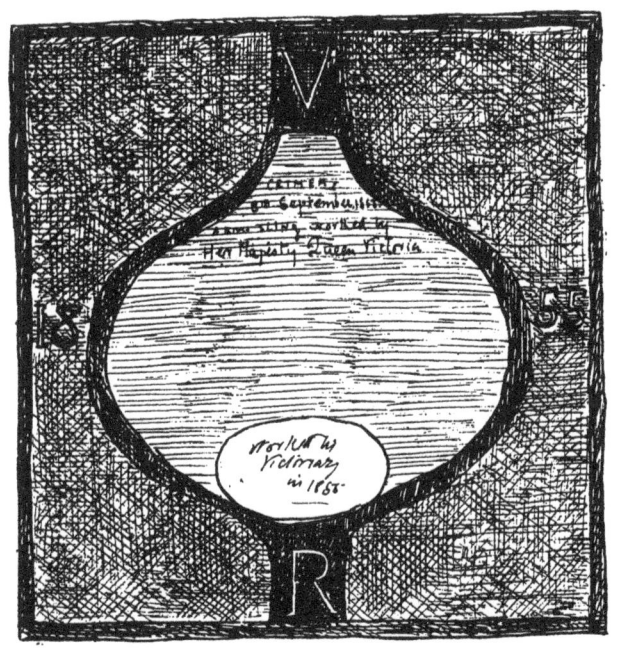

ARM SLING WORKED BY THE QUEEN.

docks—Rowlands (41st), Dewar (49th), Buchanan (47th), and Cooch (62nd). I rode all through the right attack, where I had spent so many weary nights and days. It was very strange going over the old places without the chance of being shot. I rode into the Redan by the salient angle. A road had been made through the ditch, where many poor fellows were buried, the ditch being filled up. From that I went into Sebastopol. I saw as much as I could of the ruined town. I must confess I was rather glad to get out of it, as the Russians sent some round shot from the north side during my visit. I paid Cathcart's hill a farewell visit, and saw where so many of my friends were buried.

On the 22nd of October "Bazouk" and I embarked on board the *Bahiana*. My brothers, Gustavus and Walter, saw me comfortably settled in a good cabin, said good-bye, and watched the steamer leaving Balaclava harbour. I said good-bye to the Crimea, where I spent thirteen long months; part of the time was very pleasant and part the reverse. I was only three weeks of the time absent from my regiment, when I was on board the *Columba* in Balaclava harbour, at the beginning of 1855.

There were several wounded officers on board the *Bahiana*—Lieut.-Colonel F. F. Maude, 3rd

Buffs (now Sir F. Maude, V.C., G.C.B.), Charles Henry and Barker (Royal Artillery), and Thompson (17th Regiment), I knew the best.

We stopped at Constantinople, Malta, and Gibraltar. We had a very rough time between Malta and Gibraltar, very trying to the wounded. We only steamed about two knots an hour for part of the time. Major Charles Henry (the late Lieut.-General Henry, C.B.), who lost his right arm in the trenches, used to help me to dress, and I helped him. We had two good arms between us, his left and my right, so we managed capitally.

We arrived safely at Portsmouth, very thankful to be spared to get home when so many were killed and died of disease during the campaign. It was a little disappointing to find that no one took any notice of us when we landed in our very shabby uniforms. We might as well have been ordinary travellers instead of men who had gone through the Crimean campaign.

The following short account of the 55th in the Crimea during the second winter after I left was given to me by General Sir Charles Daubeney, G.C.B., who was in command of the 55th during that time, and I am glad to add it to my Reminiscences to complete the Crimean campaign, as far as the 55th Regiment is concerned.

Sir William Codrington (Coldstream Guards) was appointed commander-in-chief of the British army in the field in succession to Sir James Simpson. In the beginning of November, 1855, Lieut.-Colonel Daubeney, who had been detained in England by order of the Government as a member of several committees on ambulance and other subjects relating to the army in the Crimea, rejoined and took command of the regiment, which was employed, all the remainder of the year, in putting up huts, &c., which were very comfortable, and a great protection to the troops during the winter, which was of unusual severity. Food and extra clothing were abundant, very different from the winter of 1854. The health of the British army was exceptionally good, a condition to which the excellent sanitary arrangements of their camps chiefly contributed. The camps of the French were in a very bad state, owing to the absence of any sanitary arrangements whatever; dead horses and other animals, and all the refuse of their camps, remaining unburied, poisoning the air. The consequence was that typhus fever broke out in the French army, and they were burying upwards of forty men daily until better arrangements were made, after the pattern of those in force in the British army. The mortality amongst the British troops was very much below the ordinary death-rate of the army at home. The Engineers were employed in blowing up the docks, forts, &c., on the south side of Sebastopol during the winter. The only exciting incident that occurred during the winter before the armistice was settled was the explosion of the English magazine to the east of the camp. It was a magnificent sight—shells and rockets were blown into the air and exploded in every direction. The 55th Regiment was employed, when the explosion took place, in levelling ground about the huts, and on other fatigue work. Lieut.-Colonel Daubeney, who was superintending the work, at once ordered the men to get their rifles, put their belts on over their fatigue clothes without waiting to put on their regular uniform, and fall in as quickly as possible. This was done so well and rapidly that the regiment was marched to the foot of the hill on which the magazine stood, and was ready, long before any others arrived, to act in case of necessity. It was not known then whether the Russians might not attempt a sudden attack on the allied position during the confusion created by the explosion. This, however, did not occur, as they were quite as much surprised as we were. Several men of the regiments encamped near the

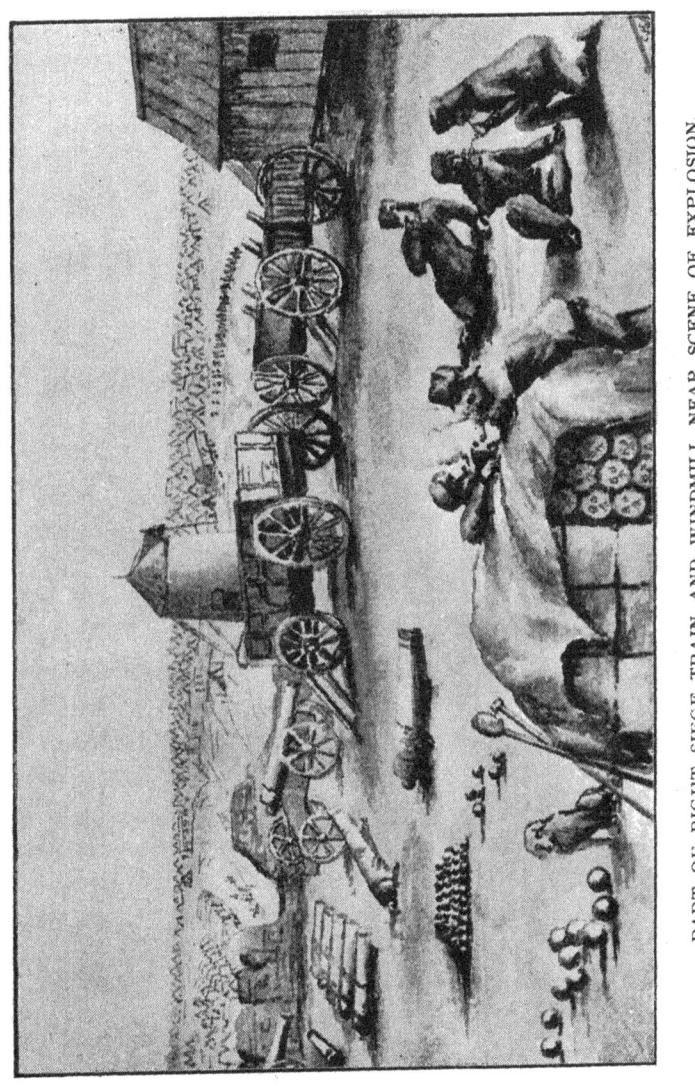

PART OF RIGHT SIEGE TRAIN AND WINDMILL NEAR SCENE OF EXPLOSION.

magazine were killed and wounded by the explosion and the pieces of shells that flew about in all directions, and several men in the hospitals were injured.

During the armistice before peace was proclaimed there was great fraternisation between the allied army and the Russians. Races and other sports were carried on during the remainder of the stay of the allied army in the Crimea, and all enjoyed the cessation of fighting. After peace was proclaimed many of the officers visited Bakshisarai and other places of interest in the Crimea; and finally the 30th and 55th Regiments embarked in one large transport, the *Great Britain*, under the command of Lieut.-Colonel Daubeney, returning to their old quarters at Gibraltar, where they were received with great enthusiasm by their old friends and the inhabitants generally.

The total of the killed, wounded, died of disease and exposure, of the 55th Regiment, from the time we left Gibraltar on the 10th of May, 1854, until the end of the war, was as follows: 6 officers, 6 sergeants, 1 drummer, 12 corporals, and 155 private soldiers, were killed or died of wounds received in battle; 6 officers, 9 sergeants, 6 corporals, and 219 privates, died of fatigue, exposure, and disease, making a total of 12 officers, 15 sergeants, 18 corporals, 1 drummer, and 374 private soldiers of the 55th Regiment, who died during the campaign of 1854-1855. In addition to the deaths above recorded, 18 officers, 1 drummer, 33 sergeants, 17 corporals, and 365 private soldiers were wounded at various times during the war ; of these, 1 officer, 3 sergeants, and 28 privates, suffered amputation. Total killed, wounded, and died of disease, of the 55th, the Westmoreland Regiment: 30 officers, 48 sergeants, 2 drummers, 35 corporals, 739 private soldiers—854 in all.

The rewards given to the 55th Regiment were not lavish. One brevet-lieut.-colonelcy and four brevet-majorities, four commissions from the ranks. Only two brevets were given to those who served through the whole siege of Sebastopol. No C.B. was given to the regiment. I was recommended for a brevet-majority, and the following is an extract from a letter of the military secretary at the time, Sir Charles Yorke :—

"I am directed by His Royal Highness to state that this officer's constant and, as he understands, meritorious services during the war had not escaped His Royal Highness's notice, and are duly recorded, but in his position among the captains of the regiment, three senior to him not having been promoted, of whom one had been severely wounded, His Royal Highness could not recommend that he should be placed over their heads, nor indeed could he add to the number of officers who have been already included in brevets, unless there should appear to be some special case of service that from any accidental circumstance, had not been previously brought to his notice."

From the above it will appear that in the Crimea it was not considered a special case of service having served though the whole siege of Sebastopol, besides being present at the battles, and after, as a captain, going through nearly nine months of trench work, leading the two front companies of the 55th, and being very severely wounded at the final assault on the Redan, and being mentioned in despatches. Of the three senior officers mentioned in the military secretary's letter, two never served in the Crimea as captains during the siege, one was on his father's staff for six weeks and then was sent home sick; the other was severely wounded, as a lieutenant, at Inkerman, and did not return to the Crimea during the siege; the third, a captain, was only a few weeks in the Crimea. I went from ensign to full colonel in the 55th, never going over the head of any one in the regiment, and never getting a brevet during my thirty years' service with the 55th. I received the Cross of the Legion of Honour in addition to the Crimean medal and three clasps, the Turkish war medal, and a medal and clasp for the Bhootan campaign, 1865, and pension for wounds.

Many changes have taken place in the army since the old Crimean days; old officers and men of the 55th and other regiments have great difficulty in recognising their dear old regiments under their new names. The 55th has been turned into the 2nd Battalion of the Border Regiment; the 34th is the 1st Battalion. If the authorities had not taken the old numbers entirely away, but had, for instance, called regiments by their new titles, retaining the old numbers, *e.g.*, 34th, 1st Battalion Border Regiment, 55th, 2nd Battalion Border Regiment, we would have been satisfied, and the individuality of the old regiments would not have been destroyed; there would be no necessity to put the numbers on the ornaments or accoutrements; they need only be used for parade purposes and to let people know what regiments were called in the old wars. Soon after I left the regiment, in 1879, the 55th was ordered to discontinue their old regimental march-past tune, "The Lass o' Gowrie," to which they had marched past for over one hundred years, and to replace it with "John Peel."

The old green facings were taken away. The regiment was given, as compensation, the names of battles it never took part in, to wear on the colours and cap ornaments. In fact the old 55th ceased to exist in 1880, when it was made the 2nd Battalion of the 34th Regiment, both making a new regiment called "the Border Regiment." I trust that some day the old numbers may be given back, and that the 55th in the future may have as good a record to show as the old corps that fought in China and the Crimea, as well as in America and the Low Countries.

The 55th was always a good, steady old regiment, well conducted in quarters and in the field, one of the best shooting regiments in the army for many years. It was much thought of in the Crimea as a capital working regiment. Sir Charles Daubeney, Sir Robert Hume, and I, three old commanding officers of the 55th, were at the parade of the Commissionaires at Chelsea, in June, 1892. When talking to a fine old non-commissioned officer, Sergeant-Major J. Morant, Royal Engineers, one of the corps of Commissionaires, we asked him, seeing that he was an old Crimean by his medals, to what attack he belonged during the siege of Sebastopol. He replied, "The right attack." We then asked him if he remembered the 55th Regiment. "The 55th!" said the sergeant-major. "One of the best working regiments in the right attack. The Engineers always liked to have working parties from the 55th." It was pleasant for the three old commanding officers of the 55th to hear such high praise of the dear old regiment after thirty-seven years had elapsed since the great siege of Sebastopol.

Writing nearly thirty-eight years after the Crimean campaign, many incidents have escaped my memory which would have been interesting to my old comrades and others. I will only add a short sketch of the career of the 55th until I gave up the command in 1879.

The 55th moved from Gibraltar to Ireland, under the command of Lieut.-Colonel Daubeney, C.B., in 1857. Lieut.-Colonel R. Hume got the command of the regiment in 1858, after eleven and a half years' service. He took the regiment out to India in 1863. The regiment went out round the Cape in three sailing ships. I was with the headquarters on board the *King Arthur*. We were 135 days from Portsmouth to Calcutta. Captain Twysden, one of our old Crimean officers, died on the voyage, much regretted by us all. Several men died of cholera after landing, when marching to Hazareebagh, in April, 1864. After being stationed there for six months we marched to Lucknow. In 1865 Sir Hugh Rose (the late Lord Strathnairn, G.C.B., &c.), commander-in-chief in India, selected the 55th to form part of the force under the late Sir Henry Tombs, in Bhootan. We were the best shooting regiment in the army, and did good service in the Bhootan campaign at the storming of the stockades at Dewangiri, on the 2nd of April, 1865. The regiment suffered much from fever when quartered at Dum Dum, after returning from Bhootan, and lost a number of men. We went to Lucknow from Dum Dum in the beginning of 1866, and were stationed there until 1869, when the commander-in-chief, Sir William Mansfield (the late Lord Sandhurst, G.C.B., G.C.S.I.), selected the 55th to make the new hill station of Chakrata. We marched to Umballa, and were present at the great durbar when Shere Ali met Lord Mayo, the Viceroy. The regiment was stationed at Chakrata for two and a half years, where we built houses, and made roads and gardens, making the station so successfully, that Colonel R. Hume, C.B., and the 55th, and Colonel Maunsell, C.B., and the Royal Engineers were given the thanks of the Government of India. Lord Mayo visited Chakrata and gave us the thanks on parade. From Chakrata we went to Peshawur in 1871, where we suffered much from cholera and fever. We all felt the death of Lord Mayo much, he was always most kind to my brother and me. We were at the great camp of exercise at Hassan Abdul, under Lord Napier of Magdala, in 1872–1873. We left Peshawur in 1874, and marched to Roorkee and Delhi. I got command of the 55th in 1874, succeeding my brother, who held it for sixteen years. He and I had the regiment for twenty-one years between us.

The headquarters of the 55th moved from Roorkee to join the detachment at Delhi, and we were quartered in the fort when His Royal Highness the Prince of Wales visited Delhi in 1876. Lord Napier of Magdala saw the 55th on parade in the fort at Delhi to wish them good-bye before he gave up his command in India. He was greatly pleased with the 55th, and when I thanked him for his great kindness to us on all occasions, he said, " My dear Hume, you have nothing to thank me for, I have had nothing but what has been pleasant with the 55th during my five years as commander-in-chief." Lord Napier took great interest in the regiment until he died, and he honoured me with his friendship up to the last. My brother got command of the Sangor District in 1874, holding it for three years until 1877. He got a division in 1879, and was sent up to take command of the Southern Afghanistan Field Force at Kandahar in 1880. He brought the force back to India in 1881, and received the thanks of the Government of India.

From Delhi the 55th went to Aden, and after being there a year I brought it home, after spending fourteen years in India. We were quartered in Gosport and Portsmouth until 1879, when we moved to Shorncliffe. I gave up the command of the 55th Regiment in December, 1879, after more than thirty years' happy service in it. In 1880 a number of the old officers dined with the 55th at Dover, and said good-bye to the old regiment just before it was called by its new title, "the 2nd Battalion of the Border Regiment." We still hope that the old numbers may be restored, and that if occasion offers the 55th Regiment may again be well to the front, and may add still more to its good record of service.

My dear brother, Lieut.-Colonel Sir Gustavus Hume, Lieut. of Her Majesty's Body Guard, the Gentlemen-at-Arms, the eldest of the four brothers who served together in the Crimea, died in June, 1891, to our very great sorrow. His loss was much felt by a multitude of friends; he had not an enemy in the world. The other three brothers are, as I write, alive and well. Sir Gustavus and Captain Walter Hume served with the 38th Regiment in the Indian Mutiny.

THE END.

The Gresham Press,
UNWIN BROTHERS,
CHILWORTH AND LONDON.

www.ingramcontent.com/pod-product-compliance
Lightning Source LLC
Chambersburg PA
CBHW030407100426
42812CB00028B/2860/J